(WANT TO BE THE "NEEDLE IN A
HAYSTACK" THEY'RE ALL LOOKING FOR?)

MATCHMAKER ... MATCHMAKER ...

HIRETRENDS, INC.

LEGAL SEARCH CONSULTANTS

NEW YORK • WASHINGTON, D.C. • LOS ANGELES

(T) 212-504-2777 • 202-478-0348 • 310-362-8878

(F) 212-504-2769 • 202-478-0303 • 310-362-8888

www.hiretrends.com

The media's watching Vault!
Here's a sampling of our coverage.

"Lawyers looking for the scoop on the nation's biggest law firms now have a place to go."
– The Wall Street Journal

"With reviews and profiles of firms that one associate calls 'spot on', [Vault's] guide has become a key reference for those who want to know what it takes to get hired by a law firm and what to expect once they get there."
– New York Law Journal

"The best place on the web to prepare for a job search."
– Fortune

"Vault is indispensable for locating insider information."
– Metropolitan Corporate Counsel

"[Vault's guide] is an INVALUABLE Cliff's Notes to prepare for interviews."
– Women's Lawyer's Journal

"For those hoping to climb the ladder of success, [Vault's] insights are priceless."
– Money Magazine

"[Vault guides] make for excellent starting points for job hunters and should be purchased by academic libraries for their career sections [and] university career centers."
– Library Journal

VAULT GUIDE TO THE TOP NEW YORK LAW FIRMS

VAULT GUIDE TO THE TOP NEW YORK LAW FIRMS

**BROOK MOSHAN GESSER, J.D.,
AND THE STAFF OF VAULT**

Library of Congress CIP Data is available.

ISBN 1-58131-271-7

Printed in the United States of America

ACKNOWLEDGEMENTS

Vault would like to thank Matt Doull, Ahmad Al-Khaled, Lee Black, Eric Ober, Hollinger Ventures, Tekbanc, New York City Investment Fund, Globix, Hoover's, Glenn Fischer, Mark Hernandez, Ravi Mhatre, Carter Weiss, Ken Cron, Ed Somekh, Isidore Mayrock, Zahi Khouri, Sana Sabbagh, and other Vault investors, as well as our family and friends.

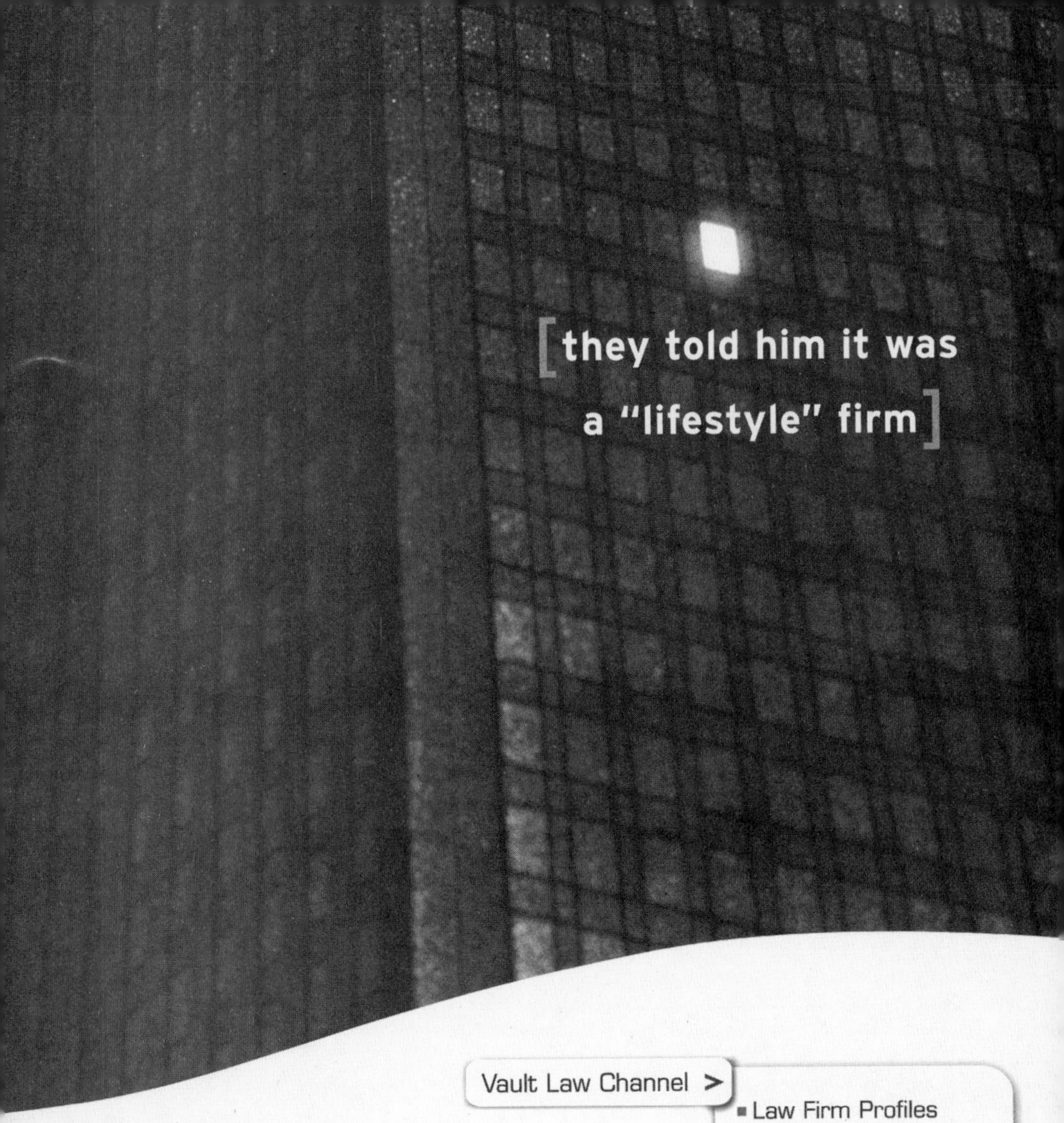
[they told him it was
a "lifestyle" firm]

LONDON CALLING

Finance/Securities 2–5 yrs exp.

Our client, one of the 'magic circle' firms in London, is interested once again in hiring U.S. attorneys. The past couple of years have been slow in London, however, this firm fared the slowdown better than most. The firm is now experiencing an impressive increase in work and is looking to hire top U.S. legal talent.

The attorneys in the Banking & Finance department of this firm work on a broad spectrum of corporate/commercial and securitization matters. This role will include a mixture of securities, derivatives, and structured finance matters, while working closely with a major U.S. Bank on restructuring transactions of domestic and international nature. There will also be an opportunity to work on general banking and project finance matters.

The ideal candidate will have between two and five years' experience gained from a 'white shoe' firm. This position offers the right candidate the opportunity to work amongst the most talented lawyers in the world, on the most sophisticated files imaginable, while living in London.

Whether you are interested in a two to three-year stint or a permanent relocation, this is a rare opportunity to change your career and your life. **For more information on this and other London positions**, please call Susan Kennedy or Salima Alibhai at the coordinates below.

Susan Kennedy or **Salima Alibhai**
1-800-410-9773
E-mail: skennedy@zsa.ca or salibhai@zsa.ca
www.zsa.ca

ZSA
LEGAL RECRUITMENT

LONDON · PARIS · HONG KONG · SYDNEY · TORONTO

Table of Contents

Limitless *Possibilities.*

Lisa*Roberts.*
Associate
Corporate Department
New York Office

The life of a first-year associate is fast-paced and can be daunting when it dawns on you how much there is to learn. In choosing Paul Hastings, I was attracted by the firm's reputation as a major player in the legal industry, but just as important to me was having access to lawyers who enjoy taking time to mentor associates. I could sense straight away that the firm had a serious and ongoing commitment to my development as a lawyer.

Paul *Hastings*

ATTORNEYS

APPENDIX   255

Introduction

Welcome to the first ever *Vault Guide to the Top New York Law Firms*. For the last six years, we've published comprehensive guides to the most prestigious law firms throughout the United States. We've realized over the years, however, that those national guides only scratched the surface of the vibrant law community in New York. So we invited associates at top New York law offices around the state to tell us about their jobs, offer suggestions to prospective associates and rate their employers on subjects such as hours, compensation, treatment by partners, training and office space. The candid assessments of New York associates regarding life at their firms are included throughout our profiles, which also contain information on major practice areas, recruiting contacts and the most notable perks each firm offers its attorneys.

We asked New Yorkers to tell us why they chose to practice in the Big Apple. The overwhelming answer was simple: "There is no better place to practice law." "New York provides the best legal training in the world," summarized one associate, while another pointed out that The City That Never Sleeps has the "biggest market" with the "best clients and work."

New York pride abounded. "I love New York!" exclaimed one jubilant attorney. "New York is the best city," said another associate, and another source explained, "I love the excitement of living and working in the city of New York." "New York City is the only U.S. city with serious culture and character," sniffed one New York fan. Proximity to Wall Street attracted countless insiders. "It's the center of the financial world," said one New Yorker, while another insisted, "New York provides the most interesting and complex corporate transactions." Old Blue Eyes explained that if you make it there, you can make it anywhere, and our survey participants agreed: "From here, you can go anywhere," noted one associate, while a smart aleck explained he is practicing here "for reasons best articulated by Frank Sinatra."

Some had more mundane reasons for choosing the Big Apple. "My family lives in the area," shrugs one New Yorker, while some say they grew up in New York City or attended law school in the Big Apple. The money's good, too, more than one associate pointed out. And the major prestige afforded lawyers of big New York law firms is nothing to sneeze at either.

Competition for positions in New York's top law firms has never been tougher, no matter which market you're considering. But rest assured: whether you're already in New York or hoping to relocate there, we're confident that, with the *Vault Guide to the Top New York Law Firms*, you'll have access to the best information to prepare yourself for interviews at the city's top firms.

A Guide to This Guide

If you're wondering how our entries are organized, read on. Here's a handy guide to the information you'll find packed into each entry of this book.

THE LAW FIRM PROFILES

Our profiles are divided into three sections: The Scoop, Getting Hired and Our Survey Says.

The Scoop: The firm's history, major clients, recent deals, major firm developments and other points of interest.

Getting Hired: Qualifications the firm looks for in new associates, tips on getting hired, information about the firm's summer associate program and other notable aspects of the hiring process.

Our Survey Says: Actual quotes from surveys and interviews with current New York associates of the firm on topics such as the firm's assignment system, work feedback, partnership prospects, levels of responsibility, summer associate program, culture, hours, compensation, training and much more.

FIRM FACTS

Locations: A listing of the firm's offices, with the headquarter office bolded. You may see firms with no bolded location. This means that these are self-proclaimed decentralized firms without official headquarters.

Major Departments/Practices: Practice areas that employ a significant portion of the firm's attorneys as reported by the firms.

Base Salary: The firm's base salary in the New York office. Pay is for 2003-2004 except where noted. Some firms have chosen not to list any salary information at all.

Notable Perks: A listing of impressive, interesting or unusual perks and benefits outside the norm. (For example, we do not list health care, as every firm we surveyed offers a health care plan.)

Uppers and Downers: Good points and bad points about working at the firm, as gleaned from associate surveys. Uppers and downers are the impressionistic perceptions of insiders and are not based on statistics.

Employment Contact: The person the firm identifies as the primary contact to receive resumes or to answer questions about the recruitment process.

THE STATS

No. of attorneys firm-wide: The total number of attorneys at a firm in all offices as of December 2003.

No. of attorneys in New York: The total number of attorneys at the firm's New York office also as of December 2003.

No. of offices: The firm's total number of offices worldwide.

Summer associate offers firm-wide: The firm-wide number of second-year law students offered full-time associate positions by the firm in 2003, as well as the number of second-year law students who participated in the firm's summer program that year.

Summer associate offers in New York: The number of second-year law students offered full-time associate positions in the New York office by the firm in 2003, as well as the number of second-year law students who participated in the firm's New York summer program that year.

Chairman, Managing Partner, etc.: The name and title of the leader of the firm. Sometimes more than one name is provided.

Hiring Partner, Hiring Attorney, etc.: The name and title of the attorney in charge of the firm's hiring efforts. Sometimes the New York hiring partner's name is given.

The Year in Law

It was the best of times, it was the worst of times? Hardly. In many ways, the year 2003 was neither here nor there for the New York legal community. Associates, weary from years of worrying about potential layoffs, were jumpy as many firms responded to the economic downturn by refusing to raise, and in some cases slashing, their year-end bonuses at the end of 2002. Twelve months later, caution was still the byword for management at the city's top firms as associates received pretty much the same bonus amount they were paid the year before. Although the now-defunct Brobeck, Phleger & Harrison was based in California, the closing of the firm's New York office in January sent disturbing shockwaves through the city's already anxious legal community.

Stand in line

A memo sent to Weil, Gotshal & Manges associates in December confirmed in print what young associates at many firms had known all along – it'll be a long time before any of them have a shot at making partner. Weil Gotshal's announcement that its partnership track would be extended to eight-and-a-half years was seen as conformation to a new industry norm; even those firms who still officially considered associates for partnerships after seven years admitted that very few candidates make it on their first round of eligibility.

But wait, it gets worse

"Engine Failure," a white paper released in September by the Center for an Urban Future, raised additional concerns about the economic future of New York City itself. Among other things, the report confirmed that September 11 scared off many young, educated people of the sort who came to New York looking for work in years past. But it turns out the terrorist attacks are actually a highly visible marker for long-running economic trends. From 1970 to 2000, for example, the city lost nearly one-third of its regional share of jobs in the finance, insurance and real estate sectors – three industries that form a critical part of any corporate law firm's client base – as existing companies took advantage of technological advances and cheaper office space to relocate outside the five boroughs and many startups also decided to try their luck elsewhere. (During that same time period, for example, northern New Jersey's share of the job market jumped 71 percent.) That may not affect Manhattan law firms too badly, since companies still want the best legal representation no matter where they keep their offices. But the legal industry isn't completely immune to the trend. Skadden, Arps, Slate, Meagher & Flom, for example, shifted 150 of its employees upstate to White Plains at the beginning of the year.

The year in securities fraud

Here's another statistic gleaned from the report: Securities and commodities brokers made 20.7 percent of the city's personal income in 2000. Three years later, though, some of the city's most prominent legal battles involved how those brokers – and their clients – made all that money. Allegations of insider trading, followed by a June indictment, kept domestic diva Martha Stewart's name in the press all year long. But don't forget that charges were also filed against Peter Bacanovic, her stockbroker at Merrill Lynch. Meanwhile, former Credit Suisse First Boston investment banker Frank Quattrone went to trial on charges of obstruction of justice for allegedly telling subordinates to destroy internal paperwork knowing full well a government investigation into the bank's distribution of technology IPO shares was underway. He managed to fight the prosecution to a standstill, however, as a deadlocked jury led to a declaration of a mistrial in late October.

White knight

One of the most prominent names in many of the cases involving financial wrongdoing was the state's attorney general, Eliot Spitzer, who was frequently cited for being even more aggressive about investigating and prosecuting securities crimes than the SEC. In September, Spitzer made headlines when his office announced a $40 million settlement with the hedge fund Canary Capital Partners, which was just one facet of an extensive probe into allegations of shady trade practices in the mutual fund industry. A month later, Spitzer teamed up with the SEC to announce the filing of a federal administrative order barring James P. Connelly, a prominent mutual fund executive, from the industry after he pled guilty to tampering with physical evidence related to the probe. Many in New York's legal community consider Spitzer the man to beat when it comes to high-profile securities cases. And the fact that Spitzer is said to have his eye on the governorship of New York only adds to his mystique.

A ray of hope

The economic news wasn't all bad, by the way. Although the first half of 2003 was the worst period for mergers and acquisitions since the mid-1990s, things turned around somewhat for the final quarter. The deals announced in that period were worth a total of $209.4 billion, nearly half of the total in M&A activity for the year. Adding to the good news, at least as far as New York attorneys were concerned, four of the top five law firms involved in the year's transactions were based in Manhattan, with Simpson Thacher & Bartlett leading the pack by advising on 71 deals worth $102.6 billion.

On the lighter side

You'd think that after all the hoopla caused by Clifford Chance's infamous associates memo of 2002, New York city law firms would have learned to be more selective about what gets put into the highly leakable print format. But in July, an associate at Paul Weiss Rifkind Wharton & Garrison was so upset with the sushi she'd ordered for an eat-in lunch that she assigned a paralegal an important task: find her a better restaurant. The paralegal compiled her research into a three-page memorandum on firm stationery, calling the sushi available through the online ordering system "mediocre at best" and highlighting other local delivery options, complete with Zagat reviews in the footnotes. "For your convenience," she noted, "I have attached each of the aforementioned menus as Exhibit 1." Nobody's sure whether the memo's thoroughness was sincere diligence or an ironic display of resentment. When the story inevitably leaked its way to the front page of the New York Times in October, no one involved was available for comment.

FIRM PROFILES

Akin Gump Strauss Hauer & Feld LLP

590 Madison Avenue
New York, NY 10022
Phone: (212) 872-1000
www.akingump.com

LOCATIONS

Albany, NY • Austin, TX •
Chicago, IL • Dallas, TX • Denver,
CO • Houston, TX • Los Angeles,
CA • McLean, VA • New York, NY
• Philadelphia, PA • Riverside, CA •
San Antonio, TX • Washington, DC
• Brussels • London • Moscow •
Riyadh (affiliate)

THE STATS

No. of attorneys firm-wide: 1,000
No. of attorneys in New York: 145
No. of offices: 16
Summer associate offers firm-wide:
71 out of 79 (2003)
**Summer associate offers in New
York:** 19 out of 20 (2003)
Chairman: R. Bruce McLean
Hiring Partner: Dennis M. Race

UPPERS

• Laid-back, familial culture
• Say bye-bye to billable hour
requirements for bonuses

DOWNERS

• Inconsistent workloads
• Lack of formal training

NOTABLE PERKS

• Yankee tickets
• Machines dispensing flavored coffee
on every floor
• Subsidized gym memberships

MAJOR DEPARTMENTS & PRACTICES

Antitrust

Corporate

Energy, Land Use &
  Environmental*

Financial Restructuring

Health Industry*

International

Intellectual Property

Investment Funds

Labor & Employment

Litigation

Public Law & Policy*

Real Estate

Tax/ERISA

White-Collar Crime

* Not a primary practice area in NY
  office

EMPOYMENT CONTACT

Ms. JeanMarie Campbell, Esq.
Legal Recruitment & Attorney
Development Manager
Fax: (212) 872-1002
E-mail: nylegalrecruiting@akingump.com

BASE SALARY

New York, NY
1st year: $125,000
Summer associate: $2,400/week

THE SCOOP

Founded in 1945 in Dallas, Texas, by former FBI agents Richard Gump and Robert Strauss, Akin Gump Strauss Hauer & Feld is now known as a prestigious Washington firm with political connections. The firm boasts respected labor, litigation, corporate and restructuring practices and has 1,000 lawyers in 16 offices (including three international locations, as well as an affiliate office in Riyadh, Saudi Arabia). Akin Gump opened a New York office in 1993, which is now the firm's second largest.

Akin Gump's litigation department has won a handful of impressive victories recently. In October 2002, a federal jury ruled in favor of Akin Gump client Kinetic Concepts, a hospital bed manufacturer. The $173 million verdict was one of the largest antitrust awards in history. A month later, another federal jury gave a much smaller but precedent-setting award to SESAC, a musicians' rights group. The jury ruled that two Pittsburgh radio stations played songs by SESAC musicians without authorization and awarded $1.2 million to Akin Gump's clients. The award was significant because it was the first jury trial for statutory copyright infringement.

Akin Gump boasts that its restructuring team has handled more than 80 major restructurings since 1999. The firm is representing informal debt-holder committees for Chapter 11 cases such as Adelphia Business Solutions, American Banknote and Covanta Energy as well as official committees for debt-holders of Aetna Industries, Burlington Industries and Daily Mart Convenience Stores.

GETTING HIRED

Insiders say that Akin Gump is looking for candidates who are "sincere, intense and from top-10 law schools." "The interview and call-back process is standard for a New York firm," says a source. "The firm recruits at top law schools and focuses on the personality and character of an applicant in addition to grades. The firm recruits candidates from schools in the 11-25 ranking but these candidates are expected to have exceptional grades in addition to strong personal qualities." In short, Akin Gump is looking for well-rounded candidates: "Grades and schools matter, but so do maturity and social skills," sums up one associate.

OUR SURVEY SAYS

Akin Gump's New York office has been blessed with a youth movement. "This is not your typical New York City law firm," says one source. "One of Akin Gump's strong suits is that it has a lot of relatively young partners who are centered and down-to-earth," reports a junior associate. "They are concerned about doing high-quality work, but they also know that family and leisure time are important." The firm is refreshingly devoid of deficient personalities. "You won't find many people here that you can actually dislike," says one contact.

While associates at many offices have griped about a deferred compensation scheme that holds back 10 percent of base salary until the end of the year, New York and Los Angeles associates are free from that system so the firm can stay in line with the market in those cities. (By 2004, the entire firm will discard the system.) That doesn't mean Akin Gump's pay scheme is free from glitches. "The compensation is competitive with other major New York firms," says one associate. "Bonuses have been an issue because prior to this year the firm had a minimum billable hour requirement. However, the firm has announced that the billable hour requirement has been abandoned this year, so our total compensation should be on par with all major New York firms." The firm points out that it also pays merit bonuses to select associates.

Akin Gump's New York office has been enjoying good times, which means extra work for its associates. "It's been a harder year than usual" because of a "combination of an explosion of work – mostly bankruptcy – and not enough associates," explains one source. "The work cycle often consists of extremes of ups and downs," complains one insider. The pressure to bill is not extreme, but it is there, and for litigators it comes in the form of a dreaded monthly report that "lists each attorney's billable hours that month, so everyone knows how hard everyone else is working." The firm insists the report is distributed in the spirit of candidness and includes the same data that partners receive regarding section performance.

Classroom time is lacking at Akin Gump, though efforts are being made to change that. (A firm-wide director of attorney development and training will join the firm in 2004 and a new training program will be implemented.) "Formal training is almost nonexistent, which is a problem," says a litigation associate. "Informal training is almost 100 percent of training, but the mentoring process here is taken very seriously." One source says "the firm appears to be in the process of revamping its formal training program in response to recent associate criticism."

Allen & Overy

1221 Avenue of the Americas
New York, NY 10020
Phone: (212) 610-6300
www.allenovery.com

LOCATIONS

London (HQ)
New York, NY • Amsterdam •
Antwerp • Bangkok • Beijing •
Bratislava • Brussels • Budapest •
Dubai • Frankfurt • Hamburg •
Hong Kong • Luxembourg • Madrid
• Milan • Moscow • Paris • Prague
• Rome • Shanghai • Singapore •
Tirana • Tokyo • Turin • Warsaw

THE STATS

No. of attorneys firm-wide: 2,400
No. of attorneys in New York: 120
No. of offices: 26
Summer associate offers firm-wide:
44 out of 46 (2003)
**Summer associate offers in New
York:** 17 out of 19 (2003)
Managing Partner: Mark Welling
Hiring Partner (NY): Peter Harwich
Hiring Partner (London): Daniel
Epstein

UPPERS

- International reach
- Love-fest environment

DOWNERS

- Unpredictable schedules
- Satellite feel to New York office

NOTABLE PERKS

- Subsidized gym membership
- 12 weeks maternity leave and 1
  week paternity leave
- Relocation and broker assistance
- Bar prep and exam expenses

MAJOR DEPARTMENTS & PRACTICES

Antitrust

Asset Finance

Banking & Finance

Communication, Media &
  Technology

Corporate

Debt Capital Markets

Derivatives

Employment & Pensions

Environmental

Equity Capital Markets

International Capital Markets

Latin America

Leveraged Finance

Litigation & Dispute Resolution

Mergers & Acquisitions

Project Finance

Real Estate

Restructuring

Securitizations

Tax

EMPLOYMENT CONTACTS

Ms. Elizabeth Papas
Legal Recruitment Manager
Phone: (646) 344-6633
E-mail: elizabeth.papas@allenovery.com

Ms. Jennifer Thornton
Legal Recruitment Coordinator
Phone: (646) 344-6673
E-mail:
jennifer.thornton@allenovery.com

Mr. Steven Murrell
US Law Group Recruitment Assistant
Phone: +44 (0) 20-7330-3568
E-mail: steven.murrell@allenovery.com

BASE SALARY

New York, NY
1st year: $125,000
Summer associate: $2,403/week

THE SCOOP

No matter where you are in the world, chances are you're not too far from Allen & Overy. The firm, part of London's "Magic Circle," has approximately 2,400 lawyers in 26 cities around the world, including New York, Paris, Hong Kong and Moscow. Allen & Overy handles a variety of international and cross-border matters, and the firm's restructuring and M&A practices have been singled out for praise.

George Allen and Thomas Overy founded Allen & Overy in London on the first day of 1930. The firm first established its reputation when it represented King Edward VIII when he abdicated the British throne in 1936. Allen & Overy opened its first overseas offices in 1978, in Dubai and Brussels. A New York office followed in 1985. The firm was one of the first Western law firms to move into Eastern Europe after the fall of the Soviet empire, opening outposts in Warsaw (1991), Prague (1992), Moscow and Budapest (1993).

The trophy case at Allen & Overy is getting a little crowded. In January 2002, A&O was named "Global Law Firm of the Year" by *Global Counsel 3000* and, separately, by *The Lawyer* in that publication's 2002 awards. In 2003 the firm was named "Litigation Team of the Year" and, again, "Law Firm of the Year" by *Legal Business.*

GETTING HIRED

Allen & Overy's interview process hardly deviates from the norm. "Students are interviewed on campus, and the lucky ones are flown to New York or London for an all-day session of interviews," says a lucky associate. "Academic excellence, law school prestige and personality fit are key criteria the firm focuses on when hiring new associates," reports one source. Don't forget that Allen & Overy is an international firm. "The firm seeks candidates that have demonstrated academic achievement but places equal if not greater emphasis on international experience, enthusiasm and personality," says one insider. "Candidates with second languages and who have lived and traveled abroad are most likely to be hired."

OUR SURVEY SAYS

If you listen to Allen & Overy associates, you'd think they've discovered legal paradise. "The work is top-notch and highly international, the people are interesting and very pleasant and the partners are generally humane," raves one associate. "Thus, it's a perfect place as far as law firms go." Many echo that high praise. "I can truly say that I love my job," says one insider. "I work with a great young partner who is always around to answer my questions and is never unreasonable. For the most part I get really good work and a good level of responsibility." "The firm's culture is by far the best thing about it," says one source. "Everyone is so accomplished and smart and has amazing backgrounds, yet fun!" exclaims another A&O insider.

Associates at the firm have typical complaints about their hours, but are generally satisfied. "On average, the workload is fine," says one insider. "I'd rather have more consistency with my hours, though. Some weeks are very slow. Others are crushing." The consistency issue comes up more than once. "I wish my schedule were more regular and predictable, but that's not what you sign up for at a firm," acknowledges one source. Face time is not an issue. "When there's work to do, you stay to get it done," reports one associate. "When there isn't, you leave. It's that simple. Many partners will apologize for making you work weekends, and vacation is considered sacred. As a first year, I have actually been laughed at for offering to cancel a long weekend vacation when a deal heated up." Artificial deadlines are also absent. Says one contact, "There are no 'pseudo-first-thing-in-the-morning' assignments unless the client really wants that."

There are few complaints about Allen & Overy's compensation structure; one insider notes the firm "paid Cravathian bonuses in an economic slowdown." Another observes the firm is "not a leader by any means, but I am confident that A&O will always match." New York lawyers enjoy the "standard New York compensation package and standard New York bonuses. In this down market, all lawyers in New York are overpaid for what we do – actually, that was true in the up market, too – but don't tell anyone."

Boies, Schiller & Flexner LLP

570 Lexington Avenue
16th Floor
New York, NY 10022
Phone: (212) 446-2300
www.bsfllp.com

LOCATIONS

Armonk, NY (HQ)
Albany, NY
Fort Lauderdale, FL
Hanover, NH
Hollywood, FL
Miami, FL
New York, NY
Oakland, CA
Orlando, FL
Palm Beach Gardens, FL
Short Hills, NJ
Washington, DC

THE STATS

No. of attorneys firm-wide: 174
No. of offices: 12
Managing Partners: David Boies,
Donald L. Flexner, Jonathan D.
Schiller
Hiring Partners: Robin A. Henry
(Armonk), Kirsten R. Gillibrand (NY)

UPPERS

- Cutting-edge, high-profile cases
- Immediate responsibility if you want it

DOWNERS

- "Opaque" bonus system
- Lack of formal training

NOTABLE PERKS

- Annual retreat, families included
- Occasional happy hours
- Laptops for all associates

MAJOR DEPARTMENTS & PRACTICE AREAS

Antitrust

Appellate

Arbitration

Business Crimes

Class Actions

Corporate

Employment/FLSA

Environmental

First Amendment

Health Care

Intellectual Property

Internal Investigation/Corporate
 Governance

International

Product Liability

Reorganization/Work-outs

Securities Litigation

EMPLOYMENT CONTACT

See list of hiring partners.

BASE SALARY*

Armonk, NY

1st year: $138,000

Summer associate: $2,500/week (2L),
$2,100/week (1L)

* *Salary not confirmed by firm.*

THE SCOOP

Boies, Schiller & Flexner is known for its handling of class-action lawsuits, commercial litigation and, most recently, its defense of companies and executives accused of malfeasance. But the young firm's reputation rests largely on the laurels of superstar litigator David Boies. Boies joined super-firm Cravath, Swaine & Moore soon after graduating magna cum laude from Yale Law School in 1966. He handled a number of high-profile cases at Cravath, including an antitrust case for IBM and a libel action for CBS and Mike Wallace. Boies left Cravath in 1997 and started his own firm in Armonk, N.Y., along with friend and fellow star lawyer Jonathan Schiller.

Boies' prominence (as well as the prominence of his firm) only grew in the late 1990s. He was hired as a special prosecutor in the closely watched antitrust case against Microsoft. In late 2000, Boies represented then-Vice President Al Gore in the case surrounding the disputed Florida election results; the case made its way to the U.S. Supreme Court, where Boies and Gore were defeated.

Boies Schiller currently has more than 170 lawyers in 12 offices around the nation. Recent matters include representing Qwest Communications (one of eight prominent law firms representing the company and its executives) against charges of accounting fraud and representing Court TV in its constitutional challenge of the State of New York's ban on cameras in the courtroom.

GETTING HIRED

"Only a few offers are given for the Armonk office," a senior associate at Boies Schiller notes, "in contrast to comparable Manhattan firms that may give over 80 offers." "The lawyers here are top-notch," brags one New York lawyer. "Associate hiring is very competitive." In other words, mere grades and accomplishment don't guarantee an offer. "The firm has interviewed many candidates who are superstars on paper, but if the applicant doesn't click with the interviewing partners, there is no way an offer is being extended. At the same time, candidates who are borderline on paper but excel in the interview are often offered positions."

OUR SURVEY SAYS

"Working in Armonk is phenomenal," says one associate at the home office. "There is no commute, or a reverse commute, and you are in a laid-back country environment in a state-of-the-art building which we just moved into. It's the type of place where you stroll into each other's offices to bounce ideas off each other." "Everyone works very hard," one source says, "but the relationship between attorneys is laid-back and friendly. It seems like everyone who is here wants to be with the firm." Another associate describes a "high-intensity atmosphere [that] is a function of workaholic lawyers who also want to spend time with their families."

"When you read the front page of *The Wall Street Journal* in the morning," brags a senior associate, "our cases are all over the front page." A fourth-year reports, "Even junior associates with initiative can do substantive work on important cases." A first-year agrees: "The junior associates here work hand-in-hand with the partners," he says, "and receive a tremendous amount of responsibility. You are treated as a lawyer, compared to other places where first-years spend the bulk of their time being treated as paralegals."

Associates at "The Firm That Boies Built" work hard. "With high-profile work, the hours are demanding," says one Boies Schiller associate. "But the good news is, with an ultra-casual environment and laptops, work can be done from anywhere. Working from home is a nonissue, and face time does not exist." One freshman says, "I know that I am in the office as much as many of my friends at other firms with reputations for being more relaxed. The difference is, when you come in you have work to do. So the billables can build themselves."

Boies Schiller associates give their compensation wildly high marks. "To my knowledge," says one associate, "only Wachtell offers similar total compensation." But they admit the system that determines their bonuses is "opaque" and occasionally "frustrating." "One year you may do better than market," another associate reports, while "next year you may do well below." Although base salaries are "slightly lower" than the top law firms, the incentive bonuses, "linked directly with the amount of work done," can result in windfalls of $100,000 to $200,000 at year's end and, says one source, "even higher bonuses to associates who worked on successful contingency-fee cases."

Brown Raysman Millstein Felder & Steiner LLP

900 Third Avenue
New York, NY 10022
Phone: (212) 895-2000
www.brownraysman.com

LOCATIONS

New York, NY (HQ)
Hartford, CT
Los Angeles, CA
Morristown, NJ
Uniondale, NY

THE STATS

No. of attorneys firm-wide: 224
No. of attorneys in New York: 180
No. of offices: 5
Summer associate offers firm-wide:
8 out of 8 (2003)
Summer associate offers in New York: 8 out of 8 (2003)
Managing Partners: Peter Brown, Richard Raysman, Julian Millstein
Hiring Partners: Barry Felder, Sarah Hewitt

UPPERS

- New commitment to training
- "Funky" new office space

DOWNERS

- Pay below market rates
- Tough hours

NOTABLE PERKS

- Yankees and Mets tickets
- Monthly cocktail party
- $50,000 in free life insurance
- "Great cafeteria"

MAJOR DEPARTMENTS & PRACTICES

Antitrust & Trade Regulation

Banking & Financial Services

Bioinformatics

Business & Finance

Construction Practice

Creditors' Rights & Business

E-Commerce

ERISA, Employee Benefits & Executive Compensation

Health Law

Information Technology

Information Technology in Healthcare

Labor & Employment

Life Sciences

Litigation

Outsourcing

Patent

Private Equity

Real Estate

Sports

Taxation

Trademark

Trusts & Estates

EMPLOYMENT CONTACT

Ms. Wanda Woods

Legal Recruiting Coordinator

Fax: (212) 895-2900

E-mail: legalrecruiting@brownraysman.com

BASE SALARY

New York, NY

1st year: $115,000

2nd year: $125,000

3rd year: $130,000

4th year: $135,000

5th year: $150,000

6th year: $165,000

7th year: $175,000

8th year: $180,000

Summer associate: $2,212/week

THE SCOOP

Like the Jeffersons, New York's Brown Raysman Millstein Felder & Steiner LLP is movin' on up. The mid-sized law firm's revenue grew an impressive 33.6 percent in 2002, tops among New York firms in *The American Lawyer*'s August 2003 Am Law 200 survey. Brown Raysman has approximately 220 lawyers in five offices. The firm has built on its reputation as a leader of intellectual property law to emerge as a solid general practice firm with a practice that includes technology, corporate finance, securities, M&A, commercial litigation, real estate, bankruptcy, media, life sciences, health care, trusts and estates and employment law.

Brown Raysman moved into new digs in New York in 2001, leaving behind the offices it occupied since its founding in 1979. The firm also opened its bioinformatics practice that year, focusing on the intersection of computer science and biotechnology. In 2002, Brown Raysman welcomed 46 lawyers from Baer, Marks & Upham LLP.

In March 2003, Brown Raysman was retained to help form a trade association for men's professional tennis players. The International Men's Tennis Association works with the ATP, professional tennis' governing body, on issues including financial matters, playing conditions and promotional concerns. Brown Raysman acted as counsel to Mount Sinai Hospital in New York when the hospital signed an IT contract with IBM in June 2003. Mount Sinai and two other New York hospitals paid IBM $380 million to provide technology services and infrastructure.

GETTING HIRED

Brown Raysman sends representatives from its New York and Hartford offices to recruiting events at a handful of law schools in the Northeast. The firm hits top-rated schools like Harvard, NYU, Columbia, Fordham, Cornell and Georgetown, as well as other schools like Brooklyn Law, BC, BU, St. John's, Cardozo and the University of Connecticut. The firm is looking for "well-rounded" candidates, say insiders. "[You] don't need to be the top 10 percent of the class or from the top-10 schools, but [you] must have other outstanding qualities." Those taking time off to work before law school may have an edge. "It appears the firm likes candidates with some previous work experience before law school," says one source.

OUR SURVEY SAYS

Insiders say the culture at Brown Raysman "varies among the departments and partners, but overall the atmosphere is social and friendly and the work is demanding but fair." Another source calls the firm's atmosphere "very mixed. Some partners are very stiff and formal. Some try to be laid-back." Associates seem to get along. "[My] colleagues tend to be very hardworking and professional but retain their sense of humor," says one insider. "I truly like my co-workers here."

Insiders suggest Brown Raysman is lagging – and secretive – when it comes to compensation. "We are paid below market rate for what is expected of us," complains one associate. "The firm could be more explicit about how I will be compensated for the deals I have referred," says one lawyer. Insiders take the long hours in stride. "I work very hard and put in many hours," says one attorney who feels "some pressure to bill, but probably no more than at other firms." Strangely, associates feel "occasional pressure to under-bill clients, which can theoretically have an adverse impact on a billable hour bonus." One insider complains of "working too many hours for not enough compensation."

Training at Brown Raysman is improving. "The firm recently began a long overdue training program," says one young associate who called the new program a "great first step." "The new training program has been very successful," agrees a midlevel associate. Informal training can be helpful as well. Says one contented source, "Attorneys here are very open to helping each other out when needed."

Generally, associates are pleased with the firm's new office space in New York. "It's a funky space," says one source. "Everything looks pretty much neat and clean. Not your traditional law firm décor, which is refreshing." It's a tight squeeze, though. "We just moved in, but it seems we're already close to outgrowing the space." One associate criticizes Brown Raysman's "dot-com, Jetsons décor" but admits the space is "pretty comfortable." Not everyone is so gracious. Says one source, "We have a really modern and expensive plastic conference room that no one likes to use because you can hear everything that goes on in it."

Bryan Cave LLP

1290 Avenue of the Americas
New York, NY 10104-3300
Phone: (212) 541-2000
www.bryancave.com

LOCATIONS

Chicago, IL
Irvine, CA
Jefferson City, MO
Kansas City, MO
Leawood, KS
Los Angeles, CA
New York, NY
Phoenix, AZ
St. Louis, MO
Washington, DC
Dubai, United Arab Emirates
Hong Kong
Kuwait City
London
Riyadh, Saudi Arabia
Shanghai

THE STATS

No. of attorneys firm-wide: 840+
No. of attorneys in New York: 218
No. of offices: 16
Summer associate offers firm-wide:
36 out of 42 (2003)
**Summer associate offers in New
York:** 11 out of 11 (2003)
Chairman: Walter L. Metcalfe Jr.
Hiring Chair (NY): Joel A. Levin

UPPERS

- International reach
- Reasonable hours

DOWNERS

- Underpays in some markets
- Culture still in flux after mergers

NOTABLE PERKS

- Free cell phones and BlackBerry service
- Get-to-know-you lunches with first-year associates and mentor program
- Annual summer party
- Laptop option for incoming associates

MAJOR DEPARTMENTS & PRACTICE AREAS

Antitrust/U.S. Trade
Appellate
Banking & Business Finance
Bankruptcy, Restructuring
 & Creditors' Rights
Class & Derivative Actions
Commercial Litigation
Commercial Plaintiff's Litigation
Corporate Compliance & Defense
Corporate Finance & Securities
Corporate Immigration
Employee Benefits
Entrepreneurial, Technology
 & Commercial Practice
Environmental
Government Contracts
Health Care
Intellectual Property
International
International Trade
Labor & Employment
Private Client
Product Liability
Public Finance
Real Estate Development,
Construction & Project Finance
Regulatory Affairs, Public Policy
 & Legislation
Secruities Enforcement, Compliance
 & Litigation
Tax Advice & Controversy
Transactions

EMPLOYMENT CONTACT

Ms. Donna M. Harris
Manager of Legal Recruiting
Phone: (212) 541-1114
Fax: (212) 541-4630
E-mail: donna.harris@bryancave.com

BASE SALARY

New York, NY
1st year: $125,000
Summer associate: $2,400/week

THE SCOOP

One of the 25 largest law firms in the U.S. (and the one with the largest Persian Gulf presence), Bryan Cave LLP is a monster of the Midwest. Named one of the fastest growing firms of 2002 by the *National Law Journal*, the firm has a unique structure comprised of 30 client service groups that focus on specific areas of the law or industry groups. One of the firm's major clients is the government of Kuwait, which the firm represented in suits against Saddam Hussein's Iraq regarding that country's invasion of Kuwaiti in 1990. Other major clients include Boeing, Bank of New York and Barnes & Noble.

In October 2001, Bryan Cave merged its Hong Kong practice with Jewkes Chan & Partners, an Asian corporate and commercial specialist. In July 2002, Bryan Cave merged with New York-based Robinson Silverman Pearce Aransohn & Berman. Thanks to the merger, Bryan Cave now has approximately 220+ lawyers practicing in New York. Bryan Cave has its share of political heavyweights on its roster, including former Mayor of New York Edward Koch, a partner in the (where else?) New York office, and former U.S. Senators Jack Danforth and Allan Dixon in St. Louis.

In 2003, the firm named a partner as the new director of professional resources to be fully dedicated to the professional development of its associates on a firm-wide basis. It also launched a mentor program and created a professional development conference for new associates.

GETTING HIRED

According to our sources, Bryan Cave is looking for "high-achieving and ambitious students who can get along with the attorneys and staff." The balance of smarts and personality is a recurring theme. "Bryan Cave is looking not only for someone who is intelligent, but also someone who can work as a team, accept responsibility and socially interact with peers and clients," reports one contact. Grades are important. "The firm has very high academic standards, and won't even talk to you if you're not at the top of your class – no exceptions," according to one lawyer. Another source says that prospective Bryan Cave associates "must be top-25 percent at a top law school. Also, moot court or law review is necessary in most cases." The firm points out that law journal experience (not just law review) is valued, too.

OUR SURVEY SAYS

Culture at a firm as big as Bryan Cave is often hard to pin down. "The firm has a reputation as being stuffy or uptight, but I've seen a real change in that perception internally over the past three or four years," says one veteran Bryan Caver. "The firm adopted a business casual dress code a couple of years ago and that seems to contribute to a less formal atmosphere. Most people adhere to it, although some of the older partners still wear suits every day."

How has the recent New York merger affected the vibe in the Big Apple office? "My sense is that the two firms that merged – Bryan Cave and Robinson Silverman – were each truly laid-back, friendly firms," says another New York associate. "The merger has changed this. Many people have grabbed onto the merger as a chance to boost their egos, try to become powerful and in general become way too ambitious."

No one is complaining much about the hours, though. "Bryan Cave has a minimum of 1,900 hours per year," says one litigator. "The reality is, practicing in litigation this number is not all that difficult to meet. Attorneys only work on weekends if they have deadlines to meet. Face time is not a part of the firm. If your workload permits it, you are encouraged to use downtime to relax, participate in community activities or pursue your professional growth and development." Associates often breeze past that 1,900 mark without breaking a sweat. "I billed over 2,000 hours last year, but it was manageable," says one associate. "The hours were spread well over the year due to a good balance with respect to the cases on which I worked."

While most Bryan Cave associates feel the "salary is competitive" there are some complaints about compensation – including the observation that "the bonus system is horrible." Big Apple lawyers are none too thrilled with the change in the compensation system. "Salary increases are no longer lock-step and are now merit based," says one associate. "As if getting work weren't competitive enough."

Cadwalader, Wickersham & Taft LLP

100 Maiden Lane
New York, NY 10038
Phone: (212) 504-6000
www.cadwalader.com

LOCATIONS

New York, NY (HQ)
Charlotte, NC
Washington, DC
London

THE STATS

No. of attorneys firm-wide: 559
No. of attorneys in New York: 405
No. of offices: 4
Summer associate offers firm-wide:
61 out of 62 (2003)
Summer associate offers in New York: 47 out of 48 (2003)
Managing Partner: Robert O. Link Jr.
Hiring Committee Chair: Paul W. Mourning

UPPERS

- Wall Street reputation goes back 200 years
- Great perks and fringe benefits

DOWNERS

- Tough road to partnership
- Unpredictable schedules

NOTABLE PERKS

- "Mentoring budget" of $130/month for first-years
- Paid sabbatical after five years
- Oodles of tech goodies like laptops and BlackBerrys

MAJOR DEPARTMENTS & PRACTICE AREAS

Banking & Finance
Capital Markets
Corporate/Mergers & Acquisitions
Financial Restructuring
Health Care/Not-for-Profit
Insurance & Reinsurance
Litigation
Private Client
Real Estate
Tax

EMPLOYMENT CONTACT

Ms. Monica R. Brenner
Manager of Legal Recruitment
Phone: (212) 504-6044
E-mail: monica.brenner@cwt.com

BASE SALARY

New York, NY
1st year: $125,000
2nd year: $135,000
3rd year: $150,000
4th year: $170,000
5th year: $190,000
6th year: $205,000
7th year: $220,000
8th year: $235,000
Summer associate: $2,400/week

THE SCOOP

Founded in 1792, Cadwalader, Wickersham & Taft LLP is one of the oldest continuous law practices in the United States. The firm has a reputation as a Wall Street power and has over 500 lawyers in four offices, including its New York headquarters, Washington, D.C., Charlotte, N.C., and London.

The year 2002 was another banner year for Cadwalader in the field of commercial mortgage backed securities, an area in which it has been long dominant. The firm was tops in both the issuer and underwriter counsel category, according to trade publication *Commercial Mortgage Alert*. Cadwalader also had a good year in mergers and acquisitions, despite the slump in the field across the legal industry in 2002. Cadwalader was eighth in M&A advisory in 2002 (according to market research firm Thomson Financial Securities Data), up from 45th in 2001. Much of that jump was due to the firm's work for pharmaceutical company Pfizer on its $62.5 billion acquisition of Swedish firm Pharmacia. The firm's M&A department is co-chaired by Dennis Block, an *American Lawyer* "Dealmaker of the Year" and among 2002's "Hot 100" according to *The Lawyer* magazine.

Cadwalader lawyers have worked on several pro bono cases for September 11 survivors and their families. Partner Deborah Steinberg advocated on behalf of illegal immigrants who were seeking compensation from the government's fund for the families of September 11 victims and won the 2003 President's Pro Bono Service Award from the New York State Bar Association for her work.

GETTING HIRED

Cadwalader's recruiting process is standard: law school students are interviewed first on campus, then at the firm's offices. Don't expect an easy road. "Given that Cadwalader is a very prestigious law firm, it has been my experience that it is very competitive to get hired here coming straight out of law school," says one insider. The firm looks favorably on particular schools. "The firm increasingly stresses Ivy League or Chicago-NYU-Michigan-type schools and excellent grades," reports one associate. Another attorney observes: "It seems like the firm is trying to recruit Ivy League students but still looks at second-tier schools as long as students are at the very top of the class."

OUR SURVEY SAYS

In general, Cadwalader associates say the firm's culture is friendly and laid-back. "This is not a formal environment," says one New York associate. "Partners and associates interact on a professional and relaxed basis, in both work and social environments." Associates are given the chance to succeed – but had better produce. "If you can do it, they let you do it," reports one lawyer. "But if you get the chance to do it, and you blow it, you can't do it anymore."

Cadwalader's associates work hours typical for big-firm lawyers. "I am very satisfied with my schedule," says one veteran associate. "We work hard, as we should at our level, but it's never mindless or unnecessary." "The firm is a high-billing place, and a premium is put on billing above 2,000 hours," states one attorney. "A typical day is about 12 hours in the office, with 15-20 not uncommon," reveals one New Yorker. "Weekend work is typical but more flexible barring a pressing deal." For some associates, the weekend is a rumor. "I cannot remember the last time I had an entire weekend off," one tired soul complains.

Cadwalader associates seem most happy on payday. "The firm is committed to matching the market, so at least I know I will make as much as I would at any other firm," says one moneybags. Some complain the firm is watching time sheets closely. "Officially, there is no billable hours requirement, but in reality bonuses are tied to hours you billed," one contact reports. That's a bone of contention. "Although it was not specifically stated that getting a bonus was tied to billable hours, many people who did not get bonuses were told that it was because their hours weren't high enough," claims one attorney. "We were not informed of this baseline threshold from the outset – only after the fact." (The firm, however, says its policy is clear: It expects a minimum of 2,000 hours per year, including time spent on recruiting, pro bono, client development, article, speech and book preparation, and training as an instructor.) The firm does have a healthy perks program. In addition to the usual goodies, like car service and meals for those working late, the firm gives associates tech toys like laptops and BlackBerry pagers. Also, in the interest of fostering teamwork and professional growth, first-years are teamed with experienced mentors and given $130 a month to paint the town red.

Cahill Gordon & Reindel LLP

80 Pine Street
New York, NY 10005
Phone: (212) 701-3000
www.cahill.com

LOCATIONS

New York, NY (HQ)
Washington, DC
London

THE STATS

No. of attorneys firm-wide: 245
No. of attorneys in New York: 243
No. of offices: 3
Summer associate offers firm-wide:
29 out of 31 (2003)
Chairman: Immanuel Kohn
Hiring Partner: Roger Meltzer

UPPERS

- Famous First Amendment practice
- Free market system lets associates choose their assignments

DOWNERS

- Assignment system can lead to hours disparity
- Virtually no formal training

NOTABLE PERKS

- Free cookies
- Matches law school donations
- Monthly happy hour

MAJOR DEPARTMENTS & PRACTICE AREAS

Antitrust
Corporate
Litigation
Real Estate
Tax
Trusts & Estates

EMPLOYMENT CONTACT

Ms. Joyce A. Hilly
Hiring Coordinator
Phone: (212) 701-3901
E-mail: jhilly@cahill.com

BASE SALARY

New York, NY
1st year: $125,000
2nd year: $135,000
3rd year: $150,000
4th year: $170,000
5th year: $190,000
6th year: $210,000
7th year: $220,000
8th year: $230,000
Summer associate: $2,400/week

THE SCOOP

With approximately 250 attorneys in three offices, Cahill Gordon & Reindel LLP is strong in finance and corporate work (a historical strength), antitrust and litigation. The firm has argued several cases before the U.S. Supreme Court and counts First Amendment super-lawyer Floyd Abrams among its ranks.

Cahill's First Amendment practice is renowned, and controversial cases are its specialty. The firm has represented the Brooklyn Museum of Art in a dispute with the City of New York and former Mayor Rudolph Giuliani over a controversial art exhibit; CBS in a dispute with the estate of Rev. Martin Luther King Jr. over the use of King's "I Have a Dream" speech; CNN over the right to broadcast impeachment proceedings against former President Clinton and U.S. Supreme Court proceedings in the 2000 election case; and Kentucky Senator Mitch McConnell in a challenge to campaign finance laws.

The firm represents some of the largest investment banks in the world, such as Credit Suisse First Boston, Deutsche Bank, Goldman Sachs, JPMorgan Chase, Merrill Lynch, Citigroup, CIBC World Markets Corp. and UBS Warburg. The firm's corporate practice extends beyond investment banks. It was part of a team that represented NBC in its $1.25 billion purchase of the Bravo cable television channel in November 2002. Cahill represented Gentiva Health Services in its January 2002 sale of its Specialty Pharmacy Division to Accredo Health.

GETTING HIRED

Applicants should know that Cahill has tweaked its hiring process. "The call-back/interview process has recently changed," says a source. "In prior years, decisions on candidates were made by one particular partner assigned to each school. Now there is an interview committee that makes hiring decisions." That committee will probably take a good, hard look at your transcripts. "In the past, Cahill has sought out a very particular type of person. Grades were far less important than personality and ability to work independently," reports one insider. "But I have heard that more emphasis is going to be put on grades going forward."

OUR SURVEY SAYS

Cahill associates describe a "laissez-faire, live and let live" culture. "If you get your work done, people don't really care about when or how you do so," says one associate. "There are no rules at Cahill, other than to do your work and do it well," observes another contact. They're serious about that one rule, though. "Partners run the firm through fear of random firings," whispers one associate. "Reviews are annual, but firings are quarterly." (Other Cahill associates made the same suggestion, which the firm strenuously denies.) That insider continues: "The firm feels that they can get away with this culture of running the firm through fear because they pay market salaries and bonuses, and the economy is rough. When the economy turns, I wouldn't be surprised if the place cleared out and many of the top associates left for firms where associates are treated decently."

Cahill's free market assignment system inspires disagreement among the associate ranks. Under the system, associates seek out the cases or deals they want to work on, rather than getting assignments from a centralized system. Supporters insist that the benefits – partners are responsible for making their cases attractive and keeping associates happy – outweigh the disadvantages. Critics of the system beg to differ, contending that uneven workloads and favoritism are unavoidable under the system. "While the firm maintains a free market system, I believe it would manage better under a coordinated workload system that so many other firms use," opines one insider. "The lack of a central assigning system means that at the same time some associates are just sitting around doing nothing, others are up to their eyeballs in work," complains another source.

Sources agree that Cahill's compensation package is "on par with other major New York law firms." "That said," says one insider, "unlike other firms in the past two years, Cahill's profits per partner continue to soar, so one might expect associates to share in that more than associates at firms where profits are down." Some associates see a discrepancy. Partners are "using the recession to justify not having to share it with those associates," fumes one lawyer. Others whine mildly that Cahill "will only match and never take the lead," a minor gripe considering the firm pays "the standard top bonus."

Carter Ledyard & Milburn LLP

2 Wall Street
New York, NY 10005
Phone: (212) 732-3200
www.clm.com

LOCATIONS

New York, NY (HQ) (two offices)
Washington, DC

THE STATS

No. of attorneys firm-wide: 125
No. of attorneys in New York: 116
No. of offices: 3
Summer associate offers firm-wide:
5 out of 5 (2003)
Summer associate offers in New York: 5 out of 5 (2003)
Managing Partner: Judith A. Lockhart
Hiring Partner: Richard G. Pierson

UPPERS

- Humane hours
- Reasonable, supportive partners

DOWNERS

- Low salary, especially for senior associates
- Firm skimps on benefits

NOTABLE PERKS

- Monthly wine and cheese parties
- Twice-weekly breakfasts
- Sports tickets
- First-year associates not assigned practice area until second year

MAJOR DEPARTMENTS & PRACTICES

Bankruptcy/Insolvency/
  Reorganization
Corporate/M&A/Securities/Private
  Equity
Employment
Environmental
Intellectual Property
Investment Management
Litigation/Arbitration
Maritime
Real Estate/Condemnation
Tax/Employee Benefits
Telecommunications
Trusts & Estates/Tax Exempt
  Organizations
White-Collar Regulatory & Defense

EMPLOYMENT CONTACT

Ms. Danielle T. Shannon
Recruitment Manager
Phone: (212) 238-8744
Fax: (212) 732-3232
E-mail: recruit@clm.com

BASE SALARY

1st year: $117,500
2nd year: $122,000
3rd year: $128,000
Summer associate: $4,896/semi-monthly

THE SCOOP

Carter Ledyard & Milburn has been a Wall Street legal fixture since its founding in 1854. A true general practice firm, the firm boasts such clients as the American Stock Exchange, Bowater Incorporated, CooperSurgical, ICAP, Liberty Media Corporation, Playtex Products, Sea Containers Ltd., Trinity Church, United States Trust Company of New York, United Business Media Corporation and the Bank of New York.

Recently, the firm acted as issuer's counsel in connection with the IPO of Orient-Express Hotels and the $360 million acquisition by Pall Corporation of the Filtration and Separations Group of USFilter Corporation. The firm is representing clients involved in the corporate investigations of Enron, Tyco and ImClone and the charges leveled against the mutual fund industry and has achieved favorable results prosecuting employment and non-solicitation agreements on behalf of Goldman Sachs and other financial industry clients. Marvel Comics looks to the firm in connection with the protection of such brands as the Incredible Hulk™ as part of the firm's growing intellectual property practice.

When Judith Lochart was elected managing partner of the firm in May 2003, she became the first woman to serve as managing partner in the firm's 150 years. She succeeded Jerome Caulfield, who remains at Carter Ledyard as a partner and a member of the executive committee.

GETTING HIRED

When it comes to hiring, Carter Ledyard prefers quiet dignity to showy pretension. "There seem to be certain common qualities that the people who are hired have – maturity and intelligence among them," observes an insider. "The firm generally does not hire people with a showy or immature attitude." Others say the firm is looking for "well-rounded individual[s] with good grades from a reputable law school." Selectivity is a key word. "The firm is extremely selective in its hiring process," says one source. "It seeks applicants from top-10 schools who match the firm's somewhat distinctive and casually conservative personality. That said, provided you go to an elite school, one need not be at the top of his or her class to be given full consideration by the hiring committee."

OUR SURVEY SAYS

Insiders say Carter Ledyard is "a humane and congenial place. Attorneys are expected to have lives outside of the office, and the workload is more than reasonable." Carter Ledyard is "both friendly and somewhat more formal than most New York firms," says a New York source. "One notices the formality mostly in that people show an unusual degree of respect for their co-workers, which extends to the secretarial and support staff. I have never heard of someone being yelled at or even someone raising his or her voice at another person." Still, some say the firm has gone through some changes recently. "The recent hiring of many lateral partners has threatened the laid-back culture. But on a whole, the core of the firm is laid-back."

Sources express lots of appreciation for the partners they work for, describing them as "very approachable, "friendly," "available" and "reasonable." And insiders say the firm is humane when it comes to hours. "The hours are very reasonable," says one insider. "There is no pressure to bill any specific number of hours," says another lawyer. "Partners are much more concerned with the quality of the work I do, rather than the number of hours I bill. I also have a lot of flexibility to choose what time I work." Shrugs one insider, "I am usually in the office at 8:30 and out by 6 – 6:30 most days."

Compensation is "the worst part of working here. There has been some talk recently among the executive committee about raising associate compensation. Bonuses are small, and base salaries don't move up much in accordance with years worked." It takes a few years for dissatisfaction to kick in. "First-year salaries are comparable to other firms, but senior associates get less here than they do at other firms," reports one attorney. "The pitch is that CLM pays a little bit less but requires fewer billables and has a much healthier lifestyle," says an insider. "That's generally true. But as associates get more and more senior, their workloads pick up much faster than their wages." Some complain the firm's health insurance is too expensive; others wish the firm matched associate 401(k) contributions.

Chadbourne & Parke LLP

30 Rockefeller Plaza
New York, NY 10112
Phone: (212) 408-5100
www.chadbourne.com

LOCATIONS

New York, NY (HQ)
Houston, TX
Los Angeles, CA
Washington, DC
Beijing
London
Moscow
Tashkent, Uzbekistan

THE STATS

No. of attorneys firm-wide: 370
No. of attorneys in New York: 278
No. of offices: 8
Summer associate offers firm-wide:
15 out of 16 (2003)
**Summer associate offers in New
York:** 15 out of 16 (2003)
Managing Partner: Charles K.
O'Neill
Hiring Partner: Vincent Dunn

UPPERS

- Prestigious project finance group
- Respectful partnership; friendly
  culture

DOWNERS

- Not enough training (except in
  litigation)
- Unpredictable hours

NOTABLE PERKS

- BlackBerrys, laptop computers on
  loan
- Free Starbucks coffee
- Online meal ordering service
- Generous subsidized gym
  membership

MAJOR DEPARTMENTS & PRACTICES

Bankruptcy
Corporate
Employment
Environmental
Intellectual Property
Litigation
Products Liability
Project Finance
Real Estate
Reinsurance/Insurance
Tax
Trusts & Estates

EMPLOYMENT CONTACT

Ms. Bernadette L. Miles
Director of Legal Recruiting
Phone: (212) 408-5338
Fax: (212) 541-5369
E-mail: bmiles@chadbourne.com

BASE SALARY

New York, NY
1st year: $125,000
2nd year: $135,000
3rd year: $150,000
4th year: $170,000
5th year: $190,000
6th year: $205,000
7th year: $210,000
8th year: $215,000
Summer associate: $2,403/week

THE SCOOP

New York-based Chadbourne & Parke LLP has approximately 370 attorneys in eight offices worldwide, 70 percent of whom are located in the firm's Rockefeller Plaza headquarters. Not afraid to court controversy, the firm has represented tobacco companies like Brown & Williamson in product liability cases and successfully defended booze maker Jim Beam in the first fetal alcohol syndrome lawsuit. Chadbourne also represented a nuclear bomb manufacturer in litigation claims filed by residents of the Marshall Islands stemming from hydrogen bomb tests that occurred there in 1954. These days, Chadbourne is representing Purdue Pharma, maker of pain medication OxyContin, in individual and class-action suits in 23 states.

The firm's project finance group is considered one of the world's best; *Infrastructure Journal* rated Chadbourne third among global infrastructure mandates for law firms. Engagements have included gas pipelines and power plants in Brazil and Argentina, power plants in India, Nepal, Pakistan and China, and numerous projects in former republics of the Soviet Union.

Chadbourne also handles project finance workout and restructuring engagements, a mix of project finance and bankruptcy law. The firm has represented lenders in the Orinoco Iron Project, a $1 billion Venezuelan iron project and has represented lenders to Enron, the Houston energy company that has become synonymous with bankruptcy and accounting shenanigans.

GETTING HIRED

At Chadbourne, academic pedigree matters. "Chadbourne only recruits from the *US News & World Report* top-15 law schools and some local New York law schools," observes one associate. Another insider concurs: "Chadbourne is looking for people with good grades at top schools or people with excellent grades from schools outside of the top-15 law schools." "It is all about grades here," says one smarty-pants. That may be an exaggeration; some Chadbourne-ites say personality is a factor, too. "The firm is looking for bright, team-oriented people who will be easy to work with," says one associate. The actual process is standard. "The interview process consists of an on-campus interview with one person for 20 minutes," says an associate. There's also "a callback where you meet with four people for roughly half an hour each."

OUR SURVEY SAYS

"Chadbourne is a friendly place, and many associates find that they do socialize outside of the office," says one social butterfly. "One of my favorite things about Chadbourne is the laid-back, informal, friendly yet professional atmosphere," says a second-year associate. "People are actually friends here, aside from being colleagues." Lace up your Nikes. "Junior associates tend to socialize together and genuinely like each other. It is not uncommon for a large group of associates to go out for drinks together or play basketball together on the weekends."

"Chadbourne tends to be a bit below the top-tier firms with respect to bonuses, if they can get away with it, but is never below market," says one source. "Regular compensation is equal to top-tier firms, and in some cases it is higher." It seems the longer an associate sticks around, the fatter the paycheck becomes, relative to other firms. "I am confident that Chadbourne management is committed to maintaining compensation levels equal to the top-tier of New York law firms," states a fourth-year. "At the midlevel range, Chadbourne is actually a step ahead of most New York firms."

Reports one Chadbourne associate, "While like every other firm there are periods of intense hours, they have been few and far between. There is no need for face time, and if you are not busy you are encouraged to leave early." Others agree face time is not necessary. "Working less would be wonderful, but the culture is not one in which you have to be here if you don't have work to do," says a contact. At least one young lawyer is happy with the time spent at the office. "The hours are not bad at all," says that newbie. "Coming out of law school, I was worried about being a slave to a law firm. I found this to be untrue at Chadbourne." Some complain about the "feast or famine" nature of billables at Chadbourne. "Hours are erratic," says one source. "There are days where you will bill two or three hours followed by days where you will bill 14 and up." Many have similar experiences, though it seems 14-hour days are a rarity. "It ebbs and flows," shrugs one insider.

Cleary, Gottlieb, Steen & Hamilton

One Liberty Plaza
New York, NY 10006-1470
Phone: (212) 225-2000
www.cgsh.com

LOCATIONS

New York, NY
Washington, DC
Brussels
Frankfurt
Hong Kong
London
Milan
Moscow
Paris
Rome
Tokyo

THE STATS

No. of attorneys firm-wide: 800
No. of attorneys in New York: 420
No. of offices: 11
Summer associate offers in domestic offices: 80 out of 80 (2003)
Summer associate offers in New York: 65 out of 65 (2003)
Managing Partner: Peter Karasz
Hiring Partner: Sheldon H. Alster

UPPERS

- Prestigious international practice
- Strong commitment to pro bono work

DOWNERS

- "Randomness" of assigning process
- Scant review process

NOTABLE PERKS

- Fabulous cafeteria
- Wine and cheese on Fridays (NY)
- Free weekly Spanish lessons
- Free gym membership at fancy-schmancy Equinox (NY)

MAJOR DEPARTMENTS & PRACTICE AREAS

Antitrust
Capital Markets
Corporate, Finance & Infrastructure
International Sovereign Debt &
 Privatization
Litigation
M&A
Real Estate
Tax
Trusts & Estates
Workouts & Bankruptcy

EMPLOYMENT CONTACT

Mr. Jaime E. Martinez
Manager of Legal Recruitment
Phone: (212) 225-3163
E-mail: jmartinez@cgsh.com

BASE SALARY

New York, NY
1st year: $125,000
2nd year: $135,000
3rd year: $150,000
4th year: $170,000
5th year: $190,000
6th year: $205,000
7th year: $220,000
8th year: $235,000
Summer associate: $2,404/week

THE SCOOP

Cleary, Gottlieb, Steen & Hamilton has a reputation for doing things a little differently – and they're proud of that. The firm has encouraged individuality and high ethical standards since its founding in 1946, when four partners of the Wall Street firm Root, Clark, Buckner & Ballantine set up their own shop and established a seniority system for associates that has become the standard in the legal industry.

Cleary has represented Argentina in its efforts to resolve financial disputes brought about by the government's defaulting on several bonds after the national economy tanked during a late-1990s recession. The firm advised the Chilean government on two multimillion-dollar bond issues in 2002; that same year, it began working with the Peruvian government on that nation's first international capital markets transactions in nearly eight decades, providing guidance on three deals that raised a total of $2 billion.

Cleary is also a leader in antitrust law, and the legal press has taken notice. In June 2002, London-based legal publisher Chambers & Partners named Cleary "Competition/ Antitrust International Law Firm of the Year," while an International Who's Who of Business Lawyers survey ranked the firm's European competition practice first among U.S.-based firms.

GETTING HIRED

"Getting in the door is the biggest challenge" for prospective Cleary associates. The "rigorous" selection process is geared toward finding "brilliant, well-rounded, gracious, sophisticated, socially attuned, mature, self-motivated" candidates "who would thrive in the less structured Cleary atmosphere." During callbacks, an insider reports, "attorneys are not provided with an applicant transcript and are asked basically to figure out whether the applicant will fit in with the firm culture and will be a team player." Before you can dazzle them in the interview, though, you need the grades. "We take intellectual capability very seriously and have a fairly high grade standard," boasts a senior attorney. Cleary is "very grade conscious," another associate agrees, "and primarily tends to give offers to students from a handful of law schools." But "good writers" and "great thinkers" from any law school can stand a chance, especially if they score high on the three I's: "Interesting. International. Intellectual."

OUR SURVEY SAYS

Most insiders regard the "slightly offbeat" associates at Cleary as "brilliant yet not boastful," as well as "exceptionally friendly, although one source admits, "We do have some strange birds here." Associates attest to high attendance at New York's weekly wine and cheese parties, a frequent "meeting place to determine where to go next." Moreover, "a number of marriages were started" at the firm. Cleary partners are "excellent teachers" who "expect and demand a very high level of work," but they also remember to "say please" and "try to keep you involved in the big picture instead of just assigning minutia" to junior associates.

Most sources agree Cleary offers "top of the market" salaries. The firm "does not always lead the pack," but "we quickly match whatever is out there." Cleary's "strong policy against firing associates," coupled with the "tough economy," have junior associates staying put. But for those who have been around a bit longer, the appeal of an in-house counsel position or "teaching, joining the UN, working in government or for an NGO" can be strong. "The firm is very slim on mid- and upper-level associates," one source reports, and others suggest that the litigation group has a "major, major problem" hanging on to its associates.

"Hard work fills your day," but "hours are long because the deals are exciting and top-of-the-line." Though some associates assure us that "there is definitely work to be done, despite the economic downturn," those who have been in the trenches a while will tell you "the work hours have been quite reasonable over the last two years." Several sources report no face time requirements. "Working from home is completely acceptable," says one litigator, "and everyone has a laptop and a BlackBerry to facilitate that." Another young corporate attorney knows several colleagues who "make it abundantly clear that they will not bill more than 50 hours a week," without drawing the ire of senior associates or partners.

Pro bono is "heavily emphasized" at Cleary, with hours on public service cases counting toward associates' billable hours (not that it matters much, many point out, since the lock-step bonuses aren't tied to minimum hours). "Cleary is really outstanding on this," says a junior litigator, who sees a "great level of interest in pro bono activities among both the associates and the partners. It is definitely highly valued."

Clifford Chance LLP

200 Park Avenue
New York, NY 10166
Phone: (212) 878-8000
www.cliffordchance.com

LOCATIONS

Los Angeles, CA • New York, NY •
Palo Alto, CA • San Diego, CA •
San Francisco, CA • Washington,
DC • Amsterdam • Bangkok •
Barcelona • Beijing • Berlin •
Brussels • Budapest • Dubai •
Dusseldorf • Frankfurt • Hong Kong
• London • Luxembourg • Madrid •
Milan • Moscow • Munich • Padua
• Paris • Prague • Rome • São
Paulo • Shanghai • Singapore •
Tokyo • Warsaw

THE STATS

No. of attorneys firm-wide: 3,700
No. of attorneys in New York: 451
No. of offices: 32
Summer associate offers firm-wide:
33 out of 33 (2003)
**Summer associate offers in New
York:** 21 out of 21 (2003)
Managing Partner: John K. Carroll
(The Americas)
Hiring Attorney: David Meister

UPPERS

- Glamorous, international atmosphere
- "Huge steps" taken to address
  concerns in associate memo

DOWNERS

- Little in the way of informal
  mentoring
- "Shameful" record regarding
  diversity

NOTABLE PERKS

- Two condos in Florida that
  associates can use for a week each
  year for free
- Munificent gym membership policy
- Generous technology allowance

MAJOR DEPARTMENTS & PRACTICES

Antitrust
Banking & Financial Restructuring
Complex Litigation & Trial Practice
Corporate Finance
Financial Products
Intellectual Property
International Litigation &
Reinsurance
Mergers & Acquisitions
Real Estate Finance
Securities Litigation/ White Collar
 Defense
Tax

EMPLOYMENT CONTACT

Ms. Carolyn Older Bortner, Esq.
Manager of Legal Recruiting
Phone: (212) 878-8252
Fax: (212) 878-8375
E-mail: Carolyn.bortner@cliffordchance.com

BASE SALARY

New York, NY
1st year: $125,000
2nd year: $135,000
3rd year: $150,000
4th year: $170,000
5th year: $190,000
6th year: $205,000
7th year: $220,000
8th year: $235,000
Summer associate: $2,404/week

THE SCOOP

Where in the world is Clifford Chance? Everywhere, that's where. The firm was the largest in the United Kingdom when it was formed in 1987 in London. In January 2000, Clifford Chance merged with German firm Pünder, Volhard, Weber & Axster and U.S. law power Rogers & Wells. The combined firm has 3,700 lawyers in 32 offices, including four California offices opened in July 2002 with lawyers who joined Clifford Chance from the now-defunct Brobeck, Phleger & Harrison. The New York office boasts such heavy-hitter clients as Citigroup, JPMorgan Chase, Merrill Lynch, MasterCard, Prudential and UBS. On behalf of these clients, the New York office practice is roughly one-half litigation advice and one-half transactional work.

Clifford Chance continues to garner respect in the legal community. In November 2002, the firm was named the top global law firm by 5,000 companies surveyed by *Global Counsel*. The firm was also the only law firm ranked in the PriceWaterhouseCoopers/*Financial Times* survey of most respected companies, ranking an impressive No. 3 in the financial services sector. A recent survey of the world's largest financial institutions by Boston-based consultants BTI found that Clifford Chance was the law firm most often named by Wall Street companies as their primary outside counsel.

Recently, the firm welcomed George Schieren, formerly head lawyer for Merrill Lynch's broker-dealer unit, in its securities litigation department.

GETTING HIRED

Clifford Chance is quickly building its brand in the United States, and the hiring criteria reflect the firm's growing American prestige. "The firm, in an effort to boost its elite status, has become much more selective in the recruiting process," says one second-year associate. The hiring process for first-year associates consists of an interview on campus, and, for candidates selected to continue to the next round, a half-day at a Clifford Chance office. The firm is said to look at a "wide variety of law schools." Associates say that Clifford Chance looks for "well-rounded candidates who are not only strong in their legal backgrounds but also in their ability to communicate effectively." Knowing several languages doesn't hurt either.

© 2004 Vault Inc.

OUR SURVEY SAYS

Clifford Chance has focused on its internal culture since associate dissatisfaction was laid bare in the 2002 associate memo. Insiders say they're seeing results in Clifford Chance's New York office. "Prior to the infamous memo, socializing was often limited to an attorney's departure gathering. Now, at least on a floor-by-floor basis, partners appear to be making an effort to at least appear more sociable," volunteers one New Yorker. Those looking for a social life will find one at Clifford Chance in New York. "There are always people to do things with outside of the office if you are so inclined, and it is an unwritten rule that work is not discussed during social activities," says one lawyer. One insider, however, comments that "the lack of a cafeteria or other meeting place" cuts down on workday camaraderie. This issue is being addressed: A cafeteria that seats several hundred is planned when the firm moves to the Deustche Bank building on 52nd Street in the spring of 2004.

One of the major complaints in the October 2002 memo centered on the firm's billable-hours guideline. That standard has now been lifted, to the joy and relief of many Clifford Chance associates. Raves one midlevel insider: "Good work requires long hours at any firm, but I am much more inclined to work more efficiently now that the hours requirement is gone." Another insider reports receiving a bonus while billing far less than the previous 2,420 minimum: "I got a full bonus last year on under 1,300 hours. I think they were really serious about putting their reliance on billables behind them."

Clifford Chance associates in New York are downright perky when discussing the array of perks they receive at the firm. "The gym membership program is outstanding – no initiation fee, 30 percent discount on monthly fee and then the firm pays for half of the lowered fee. Can't be beat," says one fit attorney. The firm also offers "free dinner for you and your significant other if you have the unfortunate pleasure of billing more than 250 hours in a month." The firm also possesses "two very nice condos in Florida that associates can use for a week each year for free." When it comes to compensation, most insiders are pleased, though one insider carps: "[Clifford Chance is] usually late in announcing bonuses and doesn't pay bonus until mid-February, unlike other firms who pay it in December."

Coudert Brothers

1114 Avenue of the Americas
New York, NY 10036
Phone: (212) 626-4400
www.coudert.com

LOCATIONS

New York, NY (HQ)
Los Angeles, CA • Palo Alto, CA •
San Francisco, CA • Washington,
DC • Almaty, Kazakhstan •
Antwerp • Bangkok • Beijing •
Berlin • Brussels • Budapest •
Frankfurt • Ghent, Belgium • Hong
Kong • Jakarta • London • Mexico
City • Milan • Moscow • Munich •
Paris • Prague • Rome • Shanghai •
Singapore • St. Petersburg •
Stockholm • Sydney • Tokyo

THE STATS

No. of attorneys firm-wide: 650+
No. of attorneys in New York: 142
No. of offices: 30
Chairman: David Huebner
Hiring Partner: Edward H.
Tillinghast III

UPPERS

- Truly global
- Glamorous international practice

DOWNERS

- Little formal training
- Compensation for senior associates
  lags behind market

NOTABLE PERKS

- Friday happy hours
- Subsidized gym membership
- Bonuses for snagging new clients
- Paid moving expenses

MAJOR DEPARTMENTS & PRACTICE AREAS

Antitrust/Competition
Banking & Project Finance
Corporate & Commercial
Customs & International Trade
Employment & Employee Benefits
Energy & Natural Resources
Foreign Investment
Global Insolvency & Financial
 Restructuring
Intellectual Property
Investment Funds & Managers
Life Sciences
Litigation & Arbitration
Mergers & Acquisitions
Private Equity/Venture Capital
Real Estate/Property
Securities
Tax
Technology, Media & Telecoms
Trusts & Estates

EMPLOYMENT CONTACT

Ms. Mary L. Simpson
Director of Legal Personnel
Phone: (212) 626-4400
Fax: (212) 626-4120
E-mail: simpsonm@coudert.com

BASE SALARY

New York, NY
1st year: $125,000
Summer associate: $2,404/week

THE SCOOP

With 30 offices in 18 countries around the world, Coudert Brothers is one of the few truly global law firms. The 650-lawyer firm is celebrating its 150th anniversary in 2003 and shows no signs of slowing down. Coudert's practice focuses on international law, naturally, with an emphasis on corporate and commercial clients. The firm specializes in project finance, trade regulation and telecommunications.

Coudert became the first U.S. law firm to open a French outpost when its Paris office opened in 1879. The firm was also the first American law practice to set up shop in the former Soviet Union and the first in Beijing after the Communist takeover. Another first came in 2001, when London partner Steven Beharrell was elected the first non-U.S. chairman of the firm. Beharrell was replaced in April 2003 by Los Angeles-based partner David Huebner, and Beharrell resigned from the firm's executive board in protest after the election. (He remains at the firm as a partner.)

In 2002, the firm advised the Russian government on the sale of its shares in LUKoil, the world's largest oil company, and was co-counsel in a successful multinational diversity jurisdiction case in front of the U.S. Supreme Court. Moreover, the firm boasts former U.S. Senator Gary Hart as counsel.

GETTING HIRED

Coudert Brothers is aiming high in its search for qualified associates. According to the firm web site, Coudert is seeking students in the top-10 percent of the class, and law review and law journal will help your cause. Insiders say the firm casts its net a little wider than most law firms. "While we do hire from a broader range of schools than most big firms, we still get some excellent candidates in the door," says one lawyer. "And our recent summer classes have been full of great students from great schools."

Interested candidates should also have an interest in international law. Coudert Brothers is "looking for international candidates from top schools," says one source. "You need to be in the top of your class and have some type of demonstrated interest in international law," concurs another insider.

OUR SURVEY SAYS

Different strokes for different folks at Coudert. "Unlike other Manhattan law firms, Coudert's attorneys and staff are not cast from a single mold," says one source. "You'll find all personality types at Coudert, which makes [the firm] one of the most interesting and pleasant places to work simply because you're always meeting people with different backgrounds and experiences." Coudert has a "healthy share of interesting characters," insists one source. The vibe at the firm is described as "laid-back and informal," and insiders appreciate that "young associates who demonstrate initiative get a lot of responsibility early on in their careers." Sources appreciate the intimate size of the New York office, which they insist means "you're well known within the firm."

These trying economic times have caused many a New York associate to wish for a longer workday, rather than the shorter one desired by countless associates in generations past. Lately, hours have been scarce at Coudert. "I sometimes wish there was more work to go around," muses one source. "There isn't enough work in most departments in which I'd like to work," reports one wistful corporate finance attorney. "And the work in my department seems to be slowing down." But even in boom times, Coudert Brothers has a reputation for not locking associates in the office. Notes one source, "Expectations with respect to billable hours are not as high as other Manhattan law firms." The downside? Getting a bonus is "not always easy."

When it comes to compensation, associates at Coudert are happy – almost. While first-year associates earn the requisite $125,000, their more senior counterparts earn salaries "slightly lower than market." Moreover, insiders gripe that "there is no market-dictated bonus," although "there is a sliding scale bonus beginning at 2,100 hours." But this hours-based bonus draws associate ire as well. "We make market on salary," reports one contact. "It would be nice to get a bonus that wasn't hours-based." Still, some insiders think the bonus situation is just dandy. "With bonuses," says a midlevel associate, "I was compensated as well as or better than associates at other New York firms."

Cravath, Swaine & Moore LLP

Worldwide Plaza
825 Eighth Avenue
New York, NY 10019
Phone: (212) 474-1000
www.cravath.com

LOCATIONS

New York, NY (HQ)
London

THE STATS

No. of attorneys firm-wide: 455
No. of attorneys in New York: 434
No. of offices: 2
Summer associate offers firm-wide:
84 out of 85 (2003)
Summer associate offers in New York: 84 out of 85 (2003)
Presiding Partner: Robert D. Joffe
Managing Partners: C. Allen Parker (Corporate), Richard W. Clary (Litigation)
Hiring Partners: Ronald Cami (Corporate), Julie A. North (Litigation)

UPPERS

- Cravath name equals "instant credibility"
- Sophisticated, high-level work

DOWNERS

- "Total commitment" to the firm expected
- Grim partnership prospects

NOTABLE PERKS

- Back-up child care
- Discount at Tiffany's
- Subsidized gym membership
- Free dinner and ride home after 8 p.m

MAJOR DEPARTMENTS & PRACTICE

Corporate
Litigation
Tax
Trusts & Estates

EMPLOYMENT CONTACT

Ms. Lisa A. Kalen
Associate Director of Legal Personnel
and Recruiting
Phone: (212) 474-3215
Fax: (212) 474-3225
E-mail: lkalen@cravath.com

BASE SALARY

New York, NY
1st year: $125,000
2nd year: $135,000
3rd year: $150,000
4th year: $170,000
5th year: $190,000
6th year: $205,000
7th year: $220,000
Summer associate: $2,500/week

THE SCOOP

For reputation and cache, it's hard to beat Cravath, Swaine & Moore. The super-prestigious law firm has under its belt more than 180 years of tradition, a blue-chip client list and some of the highest associate salaries in the industry. Cravath now has about 450 lawyers in New York and London. The firm's corporate, litigation and tax practices are among the best in the world.

Cravath boasts big cases for big-time clients. Cravath has been providing counsel to titans of industry since the 19th century, when the firm represented developers of America's vast railroad network. Modern corporate giants who turn to the firm for legal guidance include such heavy hitters as Time Warner, Bristol-Myers Squibb, Credit Suisse First Boston, Georgia Pacific, IBM, JPMorgan Chase and Vivendi Universal.

The firm counseled Time Warner through its $165 billion merger with America Online in 2000 and was part of the team that filed a federal antitrust suit against Microsoft on behalf of Time Warner. Cravath acted as American counsel for PricewaterhouseCoopers in the sale of its global business consulting and technology services unit to IBM for $3.5 billion and was legal adviser to international forest products specialist Weyerhauser in its $6.2 billion merger with competitor Willamette Industries in 2002.

Cravath is also defending Credit Suisse First Boston in a class-action lawsuit brought by frustrated Enron shareholders who allege that CSFB assisted Enron in hoodwinking its investors.

GETTING HIRED

It seems everyone and their mother wants to work at Cravath, so it stands to reason that "you don't get hired here unless you have outstanding grades from a highly competitive law school and strong interview skills." Moreover, associates say "the firm is looking for highly motivated individuals who will take initiative" and who are "not afraid of hard work." According to insiders, the call-back process "consists of a day of interviews with partners and associates in the department in which the interviewee has expressed an interest. Usually, the interviewee is given a decision by the end of the day."

OUR SURVEY SAYS

Insiders say the culture at Cravath is "very formal." But many associates say they like it that way. "I do not view [the firm's formality] as a negative," insists a new associate. "It's formal because the lawyers are diligent and focused on their work." Another insider says, "When the work is finished, we go home." Many Cravath associates mention that formal doesn't necessarily mean unfriendly. "The culture is respectful and friendly at work," suggests a first-year associate.

New Cravathites should be prepared to work long and hard. "More often than not the work is seven days a week," says a tired rookie. "At least the work is generally interesting," reports another source. Says a third-year insider, "The hours and the quality of work really go hand-in-hand. Although I would rather spend less time in the office, the significant amount of time corresponds with a significant amount of responsibility and challenging work." "The hours are long," shrugs a midlevel, "but one cannot say the firm ever misled anyone about that."

Cravath associates know their pay is at the "top of the market," and they know they shouldn't complain, but . . . Some contend that Cravath associates "should be getting paid more than all other New York firms," considering the firm's stellar reputation. A first-year argues, "I'm not eating Alpo anymore, but it would be nice if the firm matched Skadden's base [salary]." Some are conflicted when it comes to compensation: "We are well paid. But I'm not ashamed to admit that, what with student loans and high apartment rents and needing to live close to the office given my hours, I could use more. Of course, I could also be unemployed, so that said, I'm very happy with my compensation."

Cravathites go gaga over training at their firm. Raves a newbie, "There is no shortage of formal training. Also, the team system tends to lend itself to informal training, since there is an incentive for teams to help new associates become good associates." Insiders appreciate the training for "the topics covered, the material presented and the format of training sessions" and describe it as "high-tech, detailed and top-notch." The "very structured and comprehensive" litigation training program gets rave reviews. "We just built a beautiful courtroom used for training. All the partners get involved in the classes that are taught, and a lot of time goes into the preparation."

Curtis, Mallet-Prevost, Colt & Mosle LLP

101 Park Avenue
New York, NY 10178-0061
Phone: (212) 696-6000
www.cm-p.com

LOCATIONS

New York, NY (HQ)
Houston, TX • Newark, NJ •
Stamford, CT • Washington, DC •
Frankfurt • London • Mexico City •
Milan • Muscat, Oman • Paris

THE STATS

No. of attorneys firm-wide: 178
No. of attorneys in New York: 122
No. of offices: 11
Summer associate offers firm-wide:
12 out of 14 (2003)
**Summer associate offers in New
York:** 12 out of 14 (2003)
Chairman: George Kahale III

UPPERS

• Friendly culture
• International reach

DOWNERS

• Lagging on bonuses
• Ho-hum commitment to pro bono
  work

NOTABLE PERKS

• Bar dues
• Moving expenses up to $3,000
• Four weeks vacation

MAJOR DEPARTMENTS & PRACTICES

Admiralty
Aviation
Banking
Bankruptcy & Creditors' Rights
Employee Benefits
Environmental
Equity & Debt Offerings
Immigration & Nationality
Intellectual Property
International Arbitration
International Corporate
International Petroleum
International Private Client
Investment Management
Latin America
Life Sciences
Litigation
Mergers & Acquisitions
Mining
Private Equity & Venture Capital
Privatizations
Project Finance
Real Estate
Structured Finance
Tax
Telecommunications
Transportation
Trusts & Estates

EMPLOYMENT CONTACT

Ms. Alberta Baigent
Recruiting Director
Phone: (212) 696-6049
E-mail: abaigent@cm-p.com

BASE SALARY

New York, NY
1st year: $125,000
2nd year: $135,000
4th year: $145,000
5th year: $160,000
6th year: $170,000
7th year: $180,000
8th year: $190,000
Summer associate: $2,403.85/week

THE SCOOP

International law firm Curtis, Mallet-Prevost, Colt & Mosle LLP has blue-blood roots that go back to 1830, with the founding of a law firm in downtown Manhattan by two brothers of a respected Connecticut family. The firm now has approximately 170 lawyers in 11 offices worldwide and practices international corporate law and litigation. Curtis specialties include banking, bankruptcy, immigration, intellectual property, maritime law and tax.

Curtis expanded its Italy practice in June 2003 with the addition of two Milan-based legal boutiques. The firm's Milan operations, known as Curtis Mallet-Prevost & Gilioli, merged with Alemani & Bocchiola and Tamburini & Associati. The new Milan outpost is known as Gilioli Alemani Bocchiola Tamburini e Partners in associazione con Curtis Mallet-Prevost Colt & Mosle LLP, a mouthful in any language.

Back in the States, the firm represented the Federal Emergency Steel Loan Guarantee Board (ESLGB) when it loaned $250 million to steelmaker Wheeling-Pittsburgh Corp. The ESLGB, a federal agency that bails out struggling steel companies, agreed to the loan in July 2003. The infusion of cash rescued Wheeling-Pittsburgh from bankruptcy. Also in July 2003, Curtis represented the Government of the Sultanate of Oman in a deal with the Arabian Maritime and Navigation Services Co. Curtis lawyers in New York and Muscat, Oman, worked on the deal. The firm also worked on behalf of the Government of Oman in a $299.5 million shipbuilding contract with two Asian shipbuilding firms.

GETTING HIRED

Curtis hires 10-15 summer associates each year. Summer associates work in one of five departments – corporate/international, litigation, tax, trusts and estates or bankruptcy – and, like most firms, often join Curtis when they become full-fledged attorneys. The firm also hires LLMs with international expertise. Curtis is looking for "top law school students only for first-years and summers," according to one source. Those with interesting tales to tell are especially welcomed, as the firm favors "applicants with a varied background both in and out of the [legal] profession."

OUR SURVEY SAYS

The culture at Curtis is "friendly and informal, and some of the lawyers socialize together, including partners and associates." (Though, with such a "collegial" vibe, some wonder why there is "still no business casual except Fridays.") Generally, partners get high marks from our sources. "With few exceptions, the interaction between partners and associates is as casual and friendly as among associates," says one contact. "There are one or two yellers that are the exceptions that prove the rule," points out another, though one insider worries about "uncertainty regarding requirements for advancement."

The vibe around the office on payday is gloomy, according to our sources. "Salary reviews are hard to get, and bonuses are strictly related to billed hours," complains one associate. Another contact reports that "bonuses may lag behind the average for New York firms." At least the hours are reasonable. "There is an expectation of hard work when there is work to be done, but weekends are generally not considered just another day of the workweek," says one source. "When work in general is slow, there is no unreasonable pressure." The firm's New York associates spend their days in offices with "great views and nice décor," though "shared offices are a little tighter than some firms, but more attractive than most."

When it comes to training, insiders complain of "little to no formal training," but note that "on-the-job training is excellent due to the strong partner-associate relationships and early responsibility." The firm does offer "in-house seminars designed to meet CLE requirements." And sources appreciate that mentoring opportunities, though "informal and ad hoc," are still "very effective."

Curtis has had mixed results on the diversity front. One insider reveals that the firm has "many female associates [but] few female partners" and that "with the exception of Latinos, there are very few minority attorneys at the firm." Curtis also sends mixed signals when it comes to pro bono. "The firm appears to be committed to pro bono but when it comes time to count hours for purposes of promotion, one gets the feeling that pro bono hours, although billable, are not really counted," says a source.

Davis Polk & Wardwell

450 Lexington Avenue
New York, NY 10017
Phone: (212) 450-4000
www.dpw.com

LOCATIONS

New York, NY (HQ)
Menlo Park, CA
Washington, DC
Frankfurt
Hong Kong
London
Madrid
Paris
Tokyo

THE STATS

No. of attorneys firm-wide: 656
No. of attorneys in New York: 527
No. of offices: 9
Summer associate offers firm-wide:
81 out of 81 (2003)
**Summer associate offers in New
York:** 80 out of 80 (2003)
Managing Partner: John Ettinger
Hiring Partner: Gail Flesher

UPPERS

- High-level, sophisticated work for prestigious clients
- Relaxed work environment with "courteous, pleasant" co-workers

DOWNERS

- Sharing offices
- Perception that firm drags its feet when it comes to bonuses

NOTABLE PERKS

- Moving expenses, including broker's fees
- BlackBerry pagers
- In-house cafeteria
- Four weeks paternity leave (in addition to maternity leave)

MAJOR DEPARTMENTS & PRACTICES

Corporate
Litigation
Tax
Trusts & Estates

EMPLOYMENT CONTACT

Ms. Bonnie Hurry
Dir. of Recruiting & Legal Staff
Services
Phone: (212) 450-4144
Fax: (212) 450-5548
E-mail: bonnie.hurry@dpw.com

BASE SALARY

New York, NY
1st year: $125,000
2nd year: $135,000
3rd year: $150,000
4th year: $165,000
Summer associate: $2,400/week

THE SCOOP

One of the elite New York law firms, Davis Polk & Wardwell boasts stellar securities, litigation and corporate practices that serve an impressive list of prestigious clients. Among DPW's early clients was J.P. Morgan, which the firm still represents in its current form.

DPW has been involved in some of the most significant recent corporate transactions, including representing Comcast in its $53 billion acquisition of AT&T's broadband business, creating the nation's largest cable company. The firm also advised the underwriters of the $17.6 billion debt offering by GE and several subsidiaries, the largest-ever concurrent offering in the worldwide bond market. The firm advised JPMorgan Chase on Enron's $1.5 million DIP financing and Arthur Andersen in connection with the SEC probe of Enron's accounting practices. DPW also acted as defense counsel in the criminal proceedings against Andersen, which was ultimately convicted of obstruction of justice in connection with the destruction of much of Enron's paper trail. (The matter has been appealed.)

DPW acted as an adviser to the U.S. government in its sale of Governors Island to the State of New York. After years of congressional haggling and legal negotiations, the U.S. government sold the island to the city and state of New York in January 2003 for $1. DPW also represented Fred Wilpon, co-owner of the New York Mets, when he bought complete control of the baseball team from his partner, Nelson Doubleday, for $131 million.

GETTING HIRED

When it comes to hiring, DPW can afford to be choosy. A first-year source tells us, "While the firm has always been very selective, primarily recruiting top students at top law schools, this year the recruiting process seemed to get even more selective." Your academic record carries weight, but so does your personality and social skills. "It doesn't matter if you're No. 1 in your class. If you're unpleasant or exhibit poor judgment, you're not going to get an offer." Says one insider, "If you are a geek or an intellectual snob, forget it – even if you have the grades to prove it." Landing a call-back interview doesn't mean you'll get an offer. A corporate attorney reports, "Whereas most top law firms in New York give offers to 90-100 percent of those who get callbacks, here it is 30-50 percent."

OUR SURVEY SAYS

Insiders characterize the vibe at Davis Polk as "friendly and caring." The firm is "a very comfortable place to work," filled with "smart, smooth," "social," "cordial and collegial" people. "While sometimes a bit formal, the firm culture is very friendly and considerate. The associates, in particular, are real team players," says a fourth-year associate. "For a firm that does such high-level, high-pressure work," says a first-year, "the culture is very collegial and friendly." "We have a great time together without the whole fratty feeling that describes the socializing of associates at some other firms. I really can't say enough good things about the people here. With the rare exception, they are all very pleasant to be around," marvels another junior associate.

The hours at DPW "depend a lot on the practice group," with litigators often working the longest shifts. However, associates say that on the whole "the hours generally seem more humane than comparable firms." What's more, insiders say they "work only when needed, not just to bill." "Whenever I'm here late," says a fourth-year insider, "it's because I'm working on something interesting. And if I'm here, so are the senior lawyers and partners staffed on the same deal."

A first-year says he has a "modest but steady flow of billable work, and no one hassling me about it." Others reveal that "the corporate side has been slow" since the economy took a dive. Not everyone has it so easy. "I work quite a bit," says a fifth-year associate, "but they don't pay people $200,000 to work 9 to 5."

Associates describe their pay as "really good," "in line with other top-tier firms" and "just right." Still, "few New York associates will forget how Davis Polk's partners tried to eliminate associate bonuses in 2001." A second-year opines, "Davis Polk may do it grudgingly, but it is committed to matching and maintaining the top pay in New York other than Wachtell." Despite the bonus debacle of 2001, most insiders agree that "Davis Polk never came close to not matching its competitor firms' pay, and I doubt it would ever try and get away with paying less." While "compensation always ends up competitive with peer firms," insiders do feel "there is a perception that we tend to lag, at least in announcing bonuses."

Debevoise & Plimpton

919 Third Avenue
New York, NY 10022
Phone: (212) 909-6000
www.debevoise.com

LOCATIONS

New York, NY (HQ)
Washington, DC
Frankfurt
Hong Kong
London
Moscow
Paris
Shanghai

THE STATS

No. of attorneys firm-wide: 617
No. of attorneys in New York: 483
No. of offices: 8
Summer associate offers firm-wide:
111 out 111 (2003)
**Summer associate offers in New
York:** 106 out 106 (2003)
Presiding Partner: Martin Frederic
Evans
Hiring Partner: Michael J. Gillespie

UPPERS

• "Unparalleled commitment to pro
  bono"
• High-profile cases and name-brand
  clients

DOWNERS

• Sharing offices
• Lack of feedback/communication
  from partners

NOTABLE PERKS

• Subsidized cafeteria and bi-monthly
  lawyers' teas
• Same-sex domestic partner health
  coverage
• Free admission to the Whitney and
  American Folk Art museums, and
  Thirteen/WNET corporate
  membership
• Moving expenses, including broker's
  fees

MAJOR DEPARTMENTS & PRACTICE AREAS

Corporate

Litigation

Tax

Trusts & Estates

EMPLOYMENT CONTACT

Ms. Ethel F. Leichti

Manager of Associate Recruitment

Phone: (212) 909-6657

E-mail: recruit@debevoise.com

BASE SALARY

New York, NY

1st year: $125,000

2nd year: $135,000

3rd year: $150,000

4th year: $170,000

5th year: $190,000

6th year: $205,000

7th year: $220,000

8th year: $235,000

Summer associate: $2,400/week

THE SCOOP

Founded in 1931 by Eli Whitney Debevoise and William E. Stevenson (who won an Olympic gold medal in the 1,600-meter relay in 1924 and later served as U.S. ambassador to the Philippines), Debevoise & Plimpton has over 600 lawyers in eight offices around the world. No screamers here; the firm's pleasant culture makes it a favorite of humane lawyers with an academic bent.

Debevoise's corporate department is its largest, with more than 300 lawyers. The M&A department represents private equity firms, financial institutions, insurance companies, longtime industrial clients and investment banks in corporate mergers. In one high-profile deal, Debevoise advised NBC and GE when they signed documentation relating to the $14 billion combination of Vivendi Universal and NBC to create NBC Universal, valued at $43 billion. The firm counseled Prudential Financial in its agreement to combine its retail brokerage business with Wachovia Securities (with combined assets of $537 billion) and Dentsu in the formation of a partnership with Publicis Groupe to effect Publicis' $3 billion acquisition of Bcom3 Group.

The firm's litigation practice is prominent, too, and boasts superstar attorney Mary Jo White, former U.S. Attorney for the Southern District of New York. Debevoise litigators are providing legal counsel to such prominent companies as Global Crossing and Tyco in securities litigation, regulatory investigation and enforcement proceedings and white-collar criminal matters. And, in one of the largest mass tort cases in the country, the firm was retained by American Airlines to represent it in all litigation arising out of the September 11 terrorist attacks.

GETTING HIRED

"Debevoise is competitive," says one insider, "and the firm puts a great emphasis on law school grades. The firm, however, also highly values candidates with unique talents that are not law-related." Moreover, the firm looks beyond the numbers to find people who display "energy, passion and warmth." Some insiders think the firm's selectivity sometimes goes too far. According to a fourth-year insider, "You generally have to come from a top law school and graduate at the top of your class. I think one of the problems with the hiring process is that it tends to be too snobby, ignoring otherwise qualified candidates because they did not go to the 'right' schools."

OUR SURVEY SAYS

They're a contented bunch, those Debevoise associates. According to insiders, Debevoisians are considered "friendly and relaxed" and are "courteous with juniors and staff." Moreover, "classes are sociable, but not so tightly knit as to result in cliques. Relationships between junior and senior associates are easygoing and informal." "The culture is wonderfully collegial during working hours. It's everything its reputation suggests," says a first-year associate. Party animals, though, may want to look elsewhere, as "there doesn't seem to be much socializing outside of work." Still, the firm's "weekly lawyers' tea provides an atmosphere for socializing and, while most lawyers are serious, everyone is extremely nice and friendly." "The work has been interesting throughout," a third-year associate shares, "and, far more importantly, my peers have been a joy."

Most associates agree that they "can't complain about the money," although they're not doing cartwheels over it either. A second-year deems the salary "nothing special – just the usual New York deal. No complaints, but no bragging rights either." Maybe "Debevoise is not the market leader," concedes a senior associate, but the firm pays "the going rate – both salary and bonus – and matches the increases that their peer firms such as Cravath, Cleary and Davis Polk put in place

Debevoise insiders work hard. "Leaving before 10 p.m. feels early," confesses one tired first-year associate. But many associates take the long hours in stride. "I have to expect to work more than I'd like," reveals a third-year associate. "It just goes along with being at a New York firm." Of course, some associates wearing rose-colored glasses express satisfaction with the long days. According to a litigator, "If you have a deadline, expect to work regularly after 10 p.m. for the week before the due date. But there's definitely room for downtime, depending on how many cases you are juggling and when and if they are active."

Debevoise insiders positively swoon when it comes to the partners they work for. "The level of respect and cordiality between partners and associates is very high." Sources appreciate that the partners are "responsive" and "considerate of the associates' time and schedule." "Partners are approachable and nice in general and treat [associates] as colleagues," says one happy first-year. Some sources, though, complain that partners are "spotty" when it comes to giving feedback. A midlevel associate asks, "Is it really respectful and/or professionally responsible not to tell an associate on a regular basis how she can improve her work?"

Dewey Ballantine LLP

1301 Avenue of the Americas
New York, NY 10019
Phone: (212) 259-8000
www.deweyballantine.com

LOCATIONS

New York, NY (HQ)
Austin, TX
Houston, TX
Los Angeles, CA
East Palo Alto, CA
Washington, DC
Budapest
Frankfurt
London
Milan
Prague
Rome
Warsaw

THE STATS

No. of attorneys firm-wide: 580
No. of attorneys in New York: 350
No. of offices: 13
Summer associate offers firm-wide:
79 out of 80 (2003)
**Summer associate offers in New
York:** 63 out of 63 (2003)
Chairmen: Sanford W. Morhouse,
Morton A. Pierce
Hiring Partner: James A. FitzPatrick
Jr.

UPPERS

- Lots of responsibility from the get-go
- Respected M&A practice

DOWNERS

- Inequitable work allocation
- Layoffs and office closing have affected morale

NOTABLE PERKS

- Free dinners from SeamlessWeb ordering system
- Friday cocktail hour
- Profit-sharing program

MAJOR DEPARTMENTS & PRACTICE AREAS

Bankruptcy
Capital Markets
Corporate
Energy & Utility
Environmental
ERISA
Insurance
Intellectual Property
International Trade
Investment Management
Litigation
Mergers & Acquisitions
Project Finance
Real Estate
Structured Finance
Tax & Private Clients

EMPLOYMENT CONTACT

Ms. Nicole Gunn
Manager of Legal Recruitment
Phone: (212) 259-7050
Fax: (212) 259-6333
E-mail:
db.recruitment@deweyballantine.com

BASE SALARY

New York, NY
1st year: $125,000
2nd year: $135,000
3rd year: $150,000
4th year: $170,000
5th year: $190,000
6th year: $200,000
7th year: $205,000
8th year: $210,000
Summer associate: $2,403/week

THE SCOOP

New York's Dewey Ballantine, founded in 1909, boasts Thomas Dewey as a former partner; Dewey served three terms as governor of New York and ran for president twice, including once when *The Chicago Daily Tribune* prematurely reported that "Dewey Defeats Truman." (He didn't.) Dewey Ballantine now boasts top-notch antitrust, corporate, tax, and mergers and acquisitions practices.

The firm has seen talented lawyers come and go. In 2002, Dewey welcomed 11 partners from the IP practice of the now-defunct Brobeck, Phleger & Harrison. In January 2003, the firm announced it would shut its Hong Kong office, home to seven lawyers. In April 2003, Dewey snagged former Gibson, Dunn & Crutcher partner David Grais. In May 2003, three corporate partners from rival Thelen, Reid & Priest came aboard, and Stuart Hershfeld, the firm's head of bankruptcy, left for Ropes & Gray. But in September 2003, two prominent sports lawyers from Weil, Gotshal & Manges joined the firm, one of whom was Jeffrey Kessler who joined Harvey Kurzweil as co-chairman of the litigation department, and a month later Dewey launched its Italian practice with the opening of offices in Milan and Rome.

Discount retailer Kmart looked to Dewey Ballantine for assistance when it was time to file for bankruptcy. And the firm is representing insurance firm Travelers Indemnity in its case against the leaseholders of the World Trade Center. The firm recently scored a victory for this client, when the court ruled that the September 11 terrorist attacks were a single occurrence, rather than two separate acts.

GETTING HIRED

Dewey's recruiting process is typical of other big firms. One insider says the "interview and call-back process is very thorough. I had plenty of time during both to find out all of the information I needed and to show my best side. The callback started with a meet-and-greet with a member of the recruiting department, which was helpful in guiding me through the rest of the day." "Once you get a callback, it means they are really just looking at personality," says a contact. Your law school is very important. "The firm looks for candidates from top-25 law schools and the very top students at lower-tier schools."

OUR SURVEY SAYS

Most Dewey Ballantine associates are pleased with the Dewey vibe. "The firm's culture is excellent," says one insider. "Staff and attorneys of all levels interact informally but very respectfully. The firm management rightfully prides itself on having created and maintained a very congenial workplace." There may be some bad apples, but that doesn't necessarily ruin the bushel. Reports one associate, "[The firm] has a certain element of obnoxious personalities, which, given the sheer number of attorneys who work here, cannot be avoided. But those personalities are the exception, not the rule. While people socialize, and small pockets of close-knit friendships form, it is a firm that is generally respectful of an individual's personal and family life."

Dewey Ballantine associates complain of "either too little or too many" hours. The work assignment system draws gripes, as does inconsistent and unpredictable scheduling. "Our group tends not to dispense assignments until late in the afternoon, which leaves one sitting around for most of the day," says a corporate lawyer. Associates complain about face time. "I spend a lot of time with no work, but can't leave at 5 p.m. even if I have nothing to do," says one source. "Often I will do nothing all day and then get a pile of work at 4 p.m."

Despite taking home market pay, Dewey Ballantine associates have plenty of complaints about their compensation. "Like all firms, associates who work a lot of hours are not appropriately compensated at the end of the year," fumes one associate. "Of course, we are told that we are 'part of the long-term plans.' However, my bank will not lend to me based on that statement." Everyone acknowledges that they're taking home a lot; it's just that some feel it's not enough. "I get paid a lot, but I deserve even more," says one confident lawyer. "I'm good at what I do, damn it." Some New Yorkers feel they're being short-changed due to the high cost of living in the Big Apple. "It's much harder to live on $125,000 in New York City than it is in, say, Austin, Texas," says one associate. "There needs to be some recognition of this by the firms. Even an additional $10,000 a year would really, really help. Rent is ridiculous and eats up almost half of my take-home pay each month."

Epstein Becker & Green, P.C.

250 Park Avenue
New York, NY 10177-1211
Phone: (212) 351-4500
www.ebglaw.com

LOCATIONS

New York, NY (HQ)
Atlanta, GA
Boston, MA
Chicago, IL
Dallas, TX
Houston, TX
Los Angeles, CA
Newark, NJ
San Francisco, CA
Stamford, CT
Washington, DC

THE STATS

No. of attorneys firm-wide: 355
No. of attorneys in New York: 114
No. of offices: 11
Summer associates offers firm-wide: 10 out of 13 (2003)
Summer associates offers in New York: 3 out of 4 (2003)
Managing Partner: George P. Sape
Hiring Partner: Dean L. Silverberg

UPPERS

- Reasonable hours
- Laid-back culture

DOWNERS

- Pay way below market
- Did we mention the pay?

NOTABLE PERKS

- Part-time schedules
- Annual partners v. associates softball game in Central Park
- Bar review course and exam fees paid

MAJOR DEPARTMENTS & PRACTICES

Construction
Corporate & Securities
Employee Benefits
Government Contracts
Health Law
Immigration
Labor Employment
Litigation
Personal Planning & Elder Law
Real Estate
Tax

EMPLOYMENT CONTACT

Ms. Kalen T. Mikell
Attorney Recruiting & Training
Coordinator
Phone: (212) 351-4500
Fax: (212) 661-0989
E-mail: kmikell@ebglaw.com

BASE SALARY

New York, NY
1st year: $100,000
Summer associate: $1,923/week

THE SCOOP

Best known for its labor and employment and health law practices, Epstein Becker & Green has more than 350 lawyers practicing in 11 offices around the United States. Its largest office is in New York, with close to 115 attorneys.

In January 2003, Epstein Becker successfully took on the U.S. Navy when it appealed the Navy's decision to award a contract for services and supplies for naval bases in the Caribbean to a competitor of Epstein Becker client Burns and Roe Corp. Epstein Becker appealed the Navy's decision to the U.S. General Accounting Office (GAO), which has the final say on most government contracts. The GAO found for Burns and Roe, saying the Navy misevaluated the contracts, and ordered a reevaluation.

In July 2002, Epstein Becker merged with Houston-based Wickliff & Hall, the largest minority-owned law firm in Texas at the time. The firm is known as Epstein Becker Green Wickliff & Hall, P.C. in Texas and represents American and Mexican companies doing cross-border business.

Managing partner George Sape was knighted by the French Government in August 2001; he was given the French National Order of Merit for his work on Franco-American relations, especially for his involvement with a French-American museum, L'Opéra Français de New York.

GETTING HIRED

The New York office of Epstein Becker has not participated in on-campus recruitment programs during the last two years. "We don't do very extensive on-campus recruiting, [and] we don't have large summer classes," says one midlevel associate. At this time, the firm only considers write-in candidates. The firm prefers students in the top third of their class, and law review experience is, of course, a plus. Interest in the firm's core practice areas – health and labor law – is also desirable.

OUR SURVEYS SAYS

Although associates at Epstein Becker enjoy a fairly relaxed culture, party animals may want to look elsewhere. "It is laid-back and pretty friendly, but attorneys do not socialize outside of work," says one associate. "This is a family-oriented firm, and most people are on Metro North before it gets dark outside." "Lawyers get along very well but don't necessarily socialize together," agrees another insider. "People come in, do their work and go home." Associate/partner relations vary. "I've really lucked out here," says one frequently mentored associate. "There are certainly some partners who are not the best to work for here, but there are plenty of others who are wonderful to work with, and those happen to be some of the ones I work with. Associates are not given bad work here, they are given the work they prove they can handle, and partners talk to associates as business associates, not underlings."

When it comes to compensation, Epstein Becker lags behind. "As much as we're constantly being told how profitable the firm is, the pay is $30,000 below market," sighs one insider. "We are way below standard here [in terms of pay], but at least we don't work horrible hours," says one contact. "Don't get me wrong, the billable hours aren't too bad," says one contact. "In fact, associates backstab and fight each other to get billable work. The rest get stuck with non-billable work, for instance work that does not count toward your annual billable hours that determines your bonus." "You won't make the big bucks" at Epstein Becker, "but you will generally not work weekends and will not work late into the night," explains one insider.

While training at Epstein Becker is considered "average" and "depends on the partner you work with," associates are more positive when it comes to diversity. Insiders appreciate that "we have several women partners here, and several women stay on past their third year." The firm gets points for its efforts in racial diversity, but the results are lacking. "There are a lot of minority associates, but few minority senior associates and no minority partners in New York." Insiders are more tight-lipped when it comes to their firm's pro bono commitment, though one associate insists that there is "zero pro bono. Any non-billable time is spent on client development."

Fish & Neave

1251 Avenue of the Americas
New York, NY 10020
Phone: (212) 596-9000
www.fishneave.com

LOCATIONS

New York, NY (HQ)
Palo Alto, CA
Washington, DC

THE STATS

No. of attorneys firm-wide: 199
No. of attorneys in New York: 158
No. of offices: 3
Summer associate offers firm-wide:
16 out of 16 (2003)
**Summer associate offers in New
York:** 11 out of 11 (2003)
Managing Partner: Jesse J. Jenner
Hiring Partners: John M. Hintz,
Frances M. Lynch, Avi S. Lele

UPPERS

- Patent pros
- Early responsibility

DOWNERS

- Below-market bonuses for juniors
- Emphasis on billable hours

NOTABLE PERKS

- Slammin' keg parties
- Friday bagels
- "Swank" Christmas party

MAJOR DEPARTMENTS & PRACTICE AREAS

Counseling & Risk Management
Intellectual Property Asset
 Management
Intellectual Property Litigation
Licensing
Transactions

EMPLOYMENT CONTACT

Ms. Heather C. Fennell
Legal Recruitment Manager
Phone: (212) 596-9121
Fax: (212) 596-9090
hfennell@fishneave.com

BASE SALARY

New York, NY
1st year: $125,000
2nd year: $135,000
3rd year: $150,000
4th year: $165,000
5th year: $185,000
6th year: $200,000
7th year: $215,000
8th year: $230,.000
Summer associate: $2,400/week

THE SCOOP

There's nothing fishy about Fish & Neave's IP practice. The New York-based firm has represented inventors, innovators and industrial titans like Alexander Graham Bell, Henry Ford, Thomas Edison and the Wright Brothers. (The firm's web site features Flash animation of an early 1900s airplane, in honor of its past association with the famous flying brothers.) Fish & Neave now has 175 attorneys in three offices. The firm persevered through tough times post-September 11, cutting approximately 15 percent of its associates. Fish & Neave announced the opening of a Washington, D.C., outpost in June 2002 and snagged Roderick McKelvie, a prominent District Court judge with a reputation for IP expertise, as a partner for the new office.

F&N has earned a mantle-full of awards for its IP work. Trade publication *Managing Intellectual Property* named F&N "Patent Litigation Team of the Year" in 1999 and 2000, and *IP Worldwide* named the firm "No. 1 IP Counselor." In May 2003, legal publisher Chambers & Partners named Fish & Neave "IP Law Firm of the Year" at the company's annual awards dinner.

The firm has won patent victories for Harrah's Entertainment (January 2002), Symbol Technologies and Cognex Corp. (also January 2002), Compaq (July 2002) and Bio-Rad and Cornell Research Foundation (appearing before the European Patent Office's Board of Patent Appeals in November 2002).

GETTING HIRED

IP and patent law firms need more than talented lawyers; they need tech-smart people who can understand the complicated science behind medical and technology patents. Fish & Neave is no exception, and insiders say interested law students and lawyers with a science degree or applicable experience are especially appreciated. Some non-science types can be found at Fish & Neave, though. "Our primary practice area is patent litigation," explains one source. "Although the firm typically looks to hire lawyers with science or engineering backgrounds, we do hire some attorneys without such backgrounds." Fish & Neave recruiters do a good job getting the right candidates to the call-back round. "The firm weeds out most of the candidates prior to callbacks," says one attorney. "Most of the candidates I've interviewed on callbacks have been well qualified and seriously considered for positions."

OUR SURVEY SAYS

Insiders disagree about the culture at Fish & Neave; some report a friendly, open-door atmosphere, while others worry about cliques and political infighting. One associate says Fish & Neave is "more uptight than a dot-com boom firm, [but] more laid-back than a big general practice firm." Some worry about growing pains. "The firm has grown a lot and feels much more BigLaw than in the past," observes one veteran associate. "That being said, the culture remains friendly, if slightly uptight." Several associates reported a cliquey atmosphere reminiscent of junior high. Working groups "tend to be cliquey, with partners strongly preferring to work with their favorites over others."

Like many firms these days, Fish & Neave appears to be focusing more on billable hours. "There has been a trend in recent years to strongly emphasize billable hours and to ignore other non-billable hour requirements," reports one insider. "Additionally, because certain partners are overextended or lack time management stills, many litigation projects result in filing deadline [and] last-minute marathons." Complaints about partner management are frequent. "I'm spending about 2,200 hours in the office per year, of which no more than about 1,700 to 1,800 are truly billable to clients," says an associate. "The rest are devoted to firm administration, new business acquisition, and training of junior people." The complaints continue, even among those who don't mind the hours. "In general hours are reasonable," notes a source. "However, there are partners who are infamous for poor organization of cases that inevitably results in associates spending nights and weekends when it could have been avoided."

Junior associates at Fish & Neave have a lot to complain about come bonus time. "Although the base salary at Fish & Neave is identical to the salaries offered at the top New York law firms, the bonuses tend to lag behind," says a source. According to one source, the bonuses "range from nonexistent to above market, depending on your seniority." It's junior associates who miss out the most, with bonuses below market. "Fish has decided that first-through third-years are fungible and don't need to make market bonuses," fumes an insider. Senior associates, though, appreciate that "the bonus structure in more senior associate classes is actually above average for top-tier New York firms."

Fitzpatrick, Cella, Harper & Scinto

30 Rockefeller Plaza
New York, NY 10112-3801
Phone: (212) 218-2100
www.fitzpatrickcella.com

LOCATIONS

New York, NY (HQ)
Costa Mesa, CA
Washington, DC

THE STATS

No. of attorneys firm-wide: 158
No. of attorneys in New York: 124
No. of offices: 3
Summer associate offers firm wide:
18 out of 19 (2003)
Summer associate offers in New York: 15 out of 15 (2003)
Managing Partner: Dominick A. Conde
Hiring Partner: Michael P. Sandonato

UPPERS

- IP expertise
- Laid-back culture

DOWNERS

- Dearth of training
- No dental or vision care insurance

NOTABLE PERKS

- Free soda
- Free bottled water

MAJOR DEPARTMENTS & PRACTICES

Biotechnology
Copyrights
E-Commerce & New Media
Electronic & Computer
Technologies
Licensing & Transactions
Litigation
Patent Prosecution
Pharmaceuticals
Trademarks

EMPLOYMENT CONTACT

Ms. Kristen Leach
Director of Recruiting
E-mail: kleach@fchs.com

BASE SALARY

New York, NY
1st year: $125,000
Summer associate: $2,400/week

THE SCOOP

Fitzpatrick, Cella, Harper & Scinto rose from humble beginnings to become a respected intellectual property boutique. The firm, founded in 1971 by six lawyers, now has 160 attorneys in three offices. Fitzpatrick Cella handles IP matters for technology and medical science firms in nine practice areas, including litigation, licensing and transactions, copyrights, biotechnology and new media.

The firm successfully represented client Bristol-Myers Squibb in a patent dispute with the University of Michigan and Repligen Corp. Michigan and Repligen claimed a role in the discovery of processes in which T-cells can be used to regulate the immune system, but a federal judge ruled in September 2003 that they had not offered enough evidence to support the contention that they deserved co-inventor status on the resulting patents, which remain solely held by Bristol. The month before, the firm obtained a decision in favor of AstraZeneca concerning the infringement of its patent on Plendil, a blood pressure and angina medication.

In May 2002, Fitzpatrick Cella was the only New York-based firm to make *IP Worldwide*'s list of the top 10 firms for plaintiffs. A year later, it was ranked one of the city's top IP firms by Chambers & Partners in that legal research firm's 2003-2004 survey of legal expertise. Chambers also named founding partner Robert L. Baechtold as Manhattan's top IP lawyer.

GETTING HIRED

Fitzpatrick Cella's web site, www.fitzpatrickcella.com, includes a detailed career section with recruiting contacts for each of the firm's three offices. The firm recruits at approximately 40 law schools, from titans like Harvard, NYU, Stanford and Penn to lesser-known institutions like Pace, New York Law School and St. John's University. Second-year law students should apply soon after the beginning of the school year. The firm also hires a number of first-year law students who are encouraged to apply in December of their first year. Fitzpatrick Cella has a unique technical advisor program, in which part-time law students with advanced technical degrees or relevant industry experience advise on patent matters in exchange for salary, benefits and tuition reimbursement. Technical advisors can become full-time associates after graduation from law school.

OUR SURVEY SAYS

"The culture at Fitzpatrick is laid-back and friendly," says one associate. Another source agrees, "The associates for the most part are friendly with each other, and a few socialize." Yet some complaints have surfaced. "Management is very closed," says one insider. "It's extremely difficult to get accurate information, which usually makes the associate grapevine volatile, speculative and sometimes vicious." That source also feels Fitzpatrick Cella may be bringing in some inappropriate new hires: "In general, the people are nice and friendly, but on average, there's been an upsurge in obnoxious, two-faced backstabbing-types who are loud and have degrees from prestigious schools, but are otherwise completely uninformed and not team players."

"Most partners are nice enough," notes one source. "It really depends on the partner and the level of stress on that partner." Training isn't a source of pride. "The firm assigns mentors to incoming associates, but those mentors are laughable – young, inexperienced and still trying to hold their own by hording higher-level work," fumes one lawyer. "If you're lucky, you'll work with a more senior partner who takes a liking to you and will try to help you – and who isn't jealous or selfish about assignments."

One source finds there's "noticeably less pressure to bill" compared to general practice firms, while another says associates get "most weekends off." Another insider, however, complains "the hours are not conducive to having any kind of life outside of work." This attorney elaborates, "Some of us are really busy all the time, yet others leave regularly at 5:30. A small percentage of us definitely subsidize everyone else's salaries." As for those salaries, "we get paid market value, but have no eye or dental insurance," gripes one. "The bonus structure is also bizarre, with a discretionary longevity component and a 'combat pay' component that only kicks in if you bill over 2,400 hours – and then tops out if you bill over 2,600 hours."

Associates agree with the *Minority Law Journal*, which named Fitzpatrick Cella one of the top-10 law firms for diversity in 2002. "Associate classes are minority-heavy," observes one insider. One source says the firm could be doing more for female associates. "It's not so much that they're discriminatory, but that they're completely oblivious to the point," says that contact. "They focus on hiring women and the outer trappings of not saying sexist things, when they should be concentrating on helping women get more client contact and air time."

Fried, Frank, Harris, Shriver & Jacobson

One New York Plaza
New York, NY 10004
Phone: (212) 859-8000
www.friedfrank.com

LOCATIONS

New York, NY (HQ)
Los Angeles, CA
Washington, DC
London
Paris

THE STATS

No. of attorneys firm-wide: 550
No. of attorneys in New York: 375
No. of offices: 5
Summer associate offers firm-wide:
60 out of 63 (2003)
**Summer associate offers in New
York:** 41 out of 41 (2003)
Co-Managing Partners: Valerie Ford
Jacob, Paul M. Reinstein
Hiring Attorneys: Howard B. Adler,
David I. Shapiro, Steven J.
Steinman (New York)

UPPERS

- Pro bono leaders
- Training opportunities "coming out of our ears"

DOWNERS

- "Need more office space!"
- "Too many Friday-at-5:30 assignments"

NOTABLE PERKS

- Subsidized health club membership
- BlackBerrys for midlevel and senior associates
- Weekly cocktail parties
- Firm picks up tab for monthly meal with your mentor

MAJOR DEPARTMENTS & PRACTICES

Antitrust
Bankruptcy & Restructuring
Benefits & Compensation
Corporate
Litigation
Real Estate
Securities Regulation, Compliance
  & Enforcement
Tax
Technology & IP
Trusts & Estates

EMPLOYMENT CONTACT

Ms. Elizabeth M. McDonald, Esq.
Director of Legal Recruitment
Phone: (212) 859-8621
E-mail: elizabeth.mcdonald@friedfrank.com

BASE SALARY

New York, NY
1st year: $125,000
2nd year: $135,000
3rd year: $150,000
4th year: $168,000
5th year: $190,000
6th year: $205,000
7th year: $215,000
8th year: $220,000
Summer associate: $2,400/week

THE SCOOP

Founded in New York in the late 19th century, Fried, Frank, Harris, Shriver & Jacobson is a major player in the New York legal market. Boasting a prestigious corporate practice, the firm specializes in M&A.

Recent major engagements for the firm include the $5.3 billion acquisition of Rodamco North America NV by a consortium that includes Fried Frank's client the Rouse Company; the deal was named "Real Estate Deal of the Year" by *Institutional Investor*. The firm's bankruptcy practice helped European cable company NTL restructure more than half of its $13 billion in debt. *Investment Dealer's Digest* called the restructuring its "Overall Deal of the Year." Litigation clients include Martha Stewart Living Omnimedia, which the firm represented in securities class-action and shareholder derivative suits, and CIGNA, which the firm represented in seven putative federal securities class actions and two derivative suits.

In 2003, the firm's highly regarded real estate practice represented Max Capital Management in connection with the acquisition of a Park Avenue high rise, a transaction valued at nearly $500 million. In addition to advising on the negotiations of the property and lease managing agreements, the firm counseled Max Capital on the joint venture agreement with its investing partners in the purchase. Max Capital kept the firm busy that month, as it signed another deal, this time for a $320 million property in midtown Manhattan.

GETTING HIRED

Fried Frank has a yen for "serious academic types with personality" and "smart and quirky" attorneys with "interests outside of law." One source tells us, "The top law schools are well represented here, but there are plenty of very smart attorneys from other lower-tier schools." A senior associate advises, "Be cheerfully aggressive and self-confident in interviews." You can expect to meet with a partner during your on-campus interview and as many as five attorneys once you've been called back; a first-year cautions they "seem to rely heavily on the interviews." Another attorney observes, "Recruiting tries really hard to have candidates meet with attorneys in their areas of interest," and can arrange for interviews with minority and gay or lesbian attorneys at the candidate's request.

OUR SURVEY SAYS

Fried Frank associates are generally quite satisfied with life at their firm, perhaps because the vibe at the firm is one of acceptance and respect. "People's differences and eccentricities are more accepted" at Fried Frank, leading to "a weird hodgepodge of personalities" within the office walls. "The range of personal behavior that is acceptable is more broad" than at other firms, notes one insider, but also "more restrictive. Verbally abusive behavior [is] not tolerated, [and] people generally treat each other with a baseline of respect." There are some critics. "The work is boring, and the hours can be really long. People don't care about your other outside commitments," sighs an unsatisfied third-year associate.

"We don't just talk" about pro bono, brags a second-year, "we do." A first-year proudly notes, "I have already completed two pro bono assignments in six months." The New York office has a rotating four-month externship for associates at the Community Development Project of the Legal Aid Society. Externs primarily advise Harlem-based micro-entrepreneurs on corporate, real estate, intellectual property and tax issues. Other pro bono externships are available for summer associates.

"Sometimes I find myself wishing I could go to sleep," says a first-year, "but I never find myself wishing I were dead." Other Fried Frank associates report the hours, though they sometimes stretch "to the limits of human endurance," are "probably lower than most" comparable law firms. A third-year considers partners "conscientious about providing realistic deadlines, taking into account the private lives of associates. I rarely feel that stringent deadlines are imposed unless necessary." Some folks, though, complain bitterly about the unpredictability of the hours: "It's either nothing to do or here until all hours of the night."

When it comes to compensation, insiders agree the firm keeps up with its competitors. "Fried Frank is on scale with other large firms, though it tends to be a follower rather than a leader," observes one insider. "However, for first- and second-year associates, the firm doesn't tie bonuses to the number of billables, which takes off a ton of pressure, especially when the economy is slow."

Fried Frankers are just as delighted with the training at their firm. "There is always an opportunity to learn" at Fried Frank, with "tons of formal training" available every week. "We all have CLE credit coming out our ears!" boasts one associate, although some critics insist the training is "almost nonexistent after the first year."

Greenberg Traurig LLP

MetLife Building
200 Park Avenue
New York, NY 10166
Phone: (212) 801-9200
www.gtlaw.com

LOCATIONS

Atlanta, GA • Boca Raton, FL •
Boston, MA • Chicago, IL •
Denver, CO • Florham Park, NJ •
Fort Lauderdale, FL • Los Angeles,
CA • Miami, FL • New York, NY •
Orlando, FL • Philadelphia, PA •
Phoenix, AZ • Tallahassee, FL •
Tysons Corner, VA • Washington,
DC • West Palm Beach, FL •
Wilmington, DE • Amsterdam •
Zurich

THE STATS

No. of attorneys firm-wide:
1,000 +
No. of attorneys in New York: 230
No. of offices: 20
Summer associate offers firm-wide:
26 out of 29 (2003)
**Summer associate offers in New
York:** 7 out of 7 (2003)
President & CEO: Cesar L. Alvarez
Chairman: Larry J. Hoffman
Hiring Attorney: Stephen L.
Rabinowitz

UPPERS

- Early responsibility for associates
- Washington, Hollywood connections and clients

DOWNERS

- Culture becoming more rigid
- Formal dress policy

NOTABLE PERKS

- BlackBerry subsidies, paid service
- Profit sharing
- Bar expenses

MAJOR DEPARTMENTS & PRACTICES

Alternative Dispute Resolution • Americans with Disabilities Act • Antitrust • Appellate • Aviation & Aircraft Finance • Biotechnology • Corporate & Securities • Executive Compensation & Employee Benefits • Employment Law • Energy & Natural Resources Practice • Entertainment • Environmental • Financial Institutions • Global Business Group • Golf & Resort Group • Governmental Affairs • Government Contracts • Health Business Group • Immigration • Intellectual Property • International Trade & Customs • Land Use • Litigation • Lobbying • Public Finance • Public Infrastructure Group • Public Utility • Real Estate • Real Estate Operations • Reorganization, Bankruptcy & Restructuring • Retail • Structure Finance • Tax • Technology, Media & Telecommunications • Trust & Estates

EMPLOYMENT CONTACT

Ms. Elizabeth Lee
Legal Recruitment Manager
Fax: (212) 801-6400

BASE SALARY

New York, NY
1st year: $125,000
Summer associate: $2,404/week

THE SCOOP

Not many firms can boast connections in both Hollywood and Washington, but Greenberg Traurig can. Founded in Miami in 1967, Greenberg Traurig packs a powerful lobbying punch and also handles entertainment clients. Greenberg Traurig has in excess of 1,000 lawyers and government professionals in 20 offices worldwide, including new outposts in Amsterdam and Zurich.

The firm's New York office boasts strong practices in a number of areas. For example, Greenberg Traurig had a lead role in four of the 10 largest real estate transactions in New York in 2002, as reported by *The New York Times*. In *IP Law & Business*' "Top IP Firms" listing of 2003, GT shared the 10th spot ranking based on firms mentioned most often as IP litigation and patent prosecution counsel. In 2002, the firm shared the No. 2 ranking and was also listed as a top firm for prosecuting the Best Patents in 2002.

Meanwhile, the firm's litigation practice represented the tobacco industry in the appeal of the largest judgment in American legal history and lent a hand to President George W. Bush during the 2000 election dispute.

Cesar L. Alvarez heads Greenberg Traurig as the president and CEO and is a much-lauded legal eagle. He was named one of the "100 Most Influential Lawyers in America" by the *National Law Journal*, one of the "100 Most Influential Hispanics" by *Hispanic Business* and one of the "100 Most Powerful People in Miami and South Florida" by *Miami Business Magazine* and *South Florida CEO Magazine*.

GETTING HIRED

Prospective Greenberg Traurig associates have their work cut out for them, as hiring at the firm is getting tougher. Though one New York associate insists the New York office is normally "less selective" than the firm's other offices, he goes on to say that hiring "is getting more selective each year." "The firm looks for a combination of intelligence, ability and someone who will be able to fit in with the firm's culture and interact with clients," he explains. "Associates here get more client contact earlier on in their careers, so their social skills are part of the evaluation process."

OUR SURVEY SAYS

Greenberg Traurig associates see the firm's culture changing, and not necessarily for the better. Some know a firm that's "friendly, professional, courteous, laid-back," while others say "very aggressive and entrepreneurial" is more like it. According to one source, Greenberg Traurig is a place with "no hierarchy." But something different may be on the horizon – or already here – and suits and ties may have been the harbinger. "The firm is moving toward more formality, and associate culture is dead as a doorknob," laments one lawyer. "The recent move toward all-time business attire has cemented this attitude." (The firm points out, however, that the office continues to have casual Fridays and full-time casual during the summer.)

Associates disagree about the compensation at Greenberg Traurig. One associate calls the compensation at the firm "probably the most negative aspect of working here." Some insiders agree the pay is usually around the market, just not around the top of the market. "While the compensation is up there with other high-powered law firms of its size, it is on the lower end of that spectrum," complains one lawyer, who adds defensively, "I am not complaining about the salary." Other associates believe that the firm is "usually at the top of the market. There have been instances when our firm was behind the curve but they have usually adjusted to market fairly soon thereafter."

"The billable hour goals set by the firm are very reasonable, and the firm is very supportive of associates who make efforts to meet these goals," reports one insider. Most agree, saying the firm quite sensibly expects its big-firm lawyers to put in big-firm hours. One source feels "some pressure to keep high billable hours," noting that "[the] firm seems satisfied with the 2,000-2,100 billable hour range." "The typical work day is 8 a.m. to 8 p.m.," plus "four hours a day on the weekends," according to one source. Some hours pressure is natural, of course. Says one associate, "The work hours are very tolerable, but there is the nagging suspicion that layoffs – an ever present possibility in light of the firm's 'What have you done for me lately?' attitude – are closely linked to billable hours." (The firm disputes this characterization, pointing out that it hired 43 new attorneys in 2002.)

Hughes Hubbard & Reed LLP

One Battery Park Plaza
New York, N.Y. 10004-1482
Phone: (212) 837-6000
www.hugheshubbard.com

LOCATIONS

New York, NY (HQ)
Jersey City, NJ
Los Angeles, CA
Miami, FL
Washington, DC
Paris
Tokyo

THE STATS

No. of attorneys firm-wide: 315
No. of attorneys in New York: 186
No. of offices: 7
Summer associate offers in New York: 34 out of 34 (2003)
Chairwoman: Candace K. Beinecke
Managing Partner: Charles H. Scherer
Hiring Partners: Carolyn B. Levine, George A. Tsougarakis

MAJOR DEPARTMENTS & PRACTICES

Antitrust
Art Law
Corporate Reorganization
Employee Benefits
Entertainment & Media Law
Environmental
Financial Services
Intellectual Property & Technology
Labor & Employment
Latin America
Litigation
Pacific Basin
Personal Affairs
Product Liability
Real Estate
Tax
White-Collar Crime

EMPLOYMENT CONTACT

Lateral Hiring
Mr. Adrian Cockerill
Director of Legal Employment
Phone: (212) 837-6131
E-mail: cockeril@hugheshubbard.com

Law Student Hiring
Ms. Bianca Torres
Recruitment Coordinator
Phone: (212) 837-6057
E-mail: torres@hugheshubbard.com

BASE SALARY

New York, NY
1st year: $125,000
2nd year: $135,000
3rd year: $150,000
4th year: $165,000
5th year: $175,000
6th year: $180-185,000
7th year: $185-200,000
8th year: $190-200,000
Summer associate: $2,403/week

THE SCOOP

Hughes Hubbard & Reed prides itself on being a trailblazer of sorts. In the late 1880s, the firm's predecessor was the first to pay associates rather than have young lawyers and students serve as apprentices. Over 100 years later, Hughes Hubbard appointed Candace K. Beinecke the first female chair of a major New York firm. With 35 practice areas, Hughes Hubbard represents clients in the U.S., Europe, Latin America, the Pacific Basin, the Middle East and North Africa. The "Hughes" in Hughes Hubbard & Reed is Charles Evans Hughes Sr., twice a justice on the U.S. Supreme Court (including an 11-year stint as Chief Justice), secretary of state and unsuccessful candidate for president in 1916.

The firm's prominent M&A clients include PricewaterhouseCoopers, Viacom and Southern Union Co., and the firm has also completed numerous deals in the areas of media, transportation, pharmaceuticals and other industries. Litigation clients include Merck, Hallmark Cards, art auction house Christie's and Broadcast Music Inc., and the group does substantial product liability work and international arbitration. The firm has represented creditors in bankruptcy cases such as Enron, Renaissance Cruises, TWA, FINOVA, Wheeling-Pittsburgh, PG&E and Fruit of the Loom and represented the Federal National Mortgage Association in the restructuring of loans owed by those affected by the September 11 terrorist attacks.

In January 2003, Hughes Hubbard welcomed the New York office of Washington, D.C.-based Zuckerman Spaeder to start a white-collar practice, led by a prominent former federal prosecutor Edward Little. The firm also brought on noted international arbitrator José Rosell.

GETTING HIRED

Hughes Hubbard sources say personality is an important factor in hiring. "The interview process was friendly and not intimidating – more like they just want to get to know you, not grill you on your legal knowledge," reports one contact. "The firm seems to be looking for nice, well-rounded, easygoing, intelligent and hardworking people, whom they wouldn't mind working with in the wee hours." But pedigree and grades are still vital. "If you go to a top-five law school, it is not hard" to get hired at the firm, according to one attorney. "If not, law review is a plus." (Where is it not a plus?)

OUR SURVEY SAYS

Insiders say Hughes Hubbard's culture is "generally pretty respectful. There are always some people who can be condescending or unpleasant, but they stick out here because they are the exception." Associates appreciate the "all-attorney breakfasts and pizza-nights in the offices once a week," as well as the "reinstituted cocktail parties once a month – not just during the summer to impress the gullible." But some associates feel they were sold a culture that just isn't there. "It was originally billed as a lifestyle firm when we were recruited, which is a large part of why a lot of us came here," reports one contact. "They've been actively trying to get rid of that image and be as hard core as the other New York firms."

Hughes Hubbard associates spend their share of time at the office. "Generally, I work long hours weekdays and most weekends," says one source. Insiders point out that "the implicit billable hours requirement/expectation makes it almost imperative to spend long hours at work." Hours can vary according to department. "Much of litigation is expected to maintain a 55-hour per week minimum billable requirement," says a lawyer from that department. "That's a 2,640 minimum billable year, even if you take your full four weeks of vacation." Thanks to a sluggish economy, the hours are less intense in the corporate department. "Hours are lower this year all around, so I can't complain," says a corporate lawyer. Pressure to put in face time is scarce. "While they expect you to make yourself available for the late hours, weekend work and cancelled vacations when the matter calls for it," says one insider, "there doesn't seem to be any desire to have associates sitting at their desks at 9 p.m. every night just because. If I'm not busy, I'll leave at 6:30 without embarrassment. Without much, anyway."

Though most agree Hughes Hubbard pays "at the New York rate," there are still some complaints about the firm's salary and bonus structure. "They need to stop using the simple billables threshold model," complains one insider. "It creates inequities between divisions and is the catalyst for puffing and hoarding by senior associates who feel underpaid." Not that the associate in question is crying poverty. "We are, of course, paid extremely well relative to other sectors in the poor economy, and some people are racking up huge bonuses."

Jackson Lewis LLP

59 Maiden Lane
New York, NY 10038
Phone: (212) 545-4000
www.jacksonlewis.com

LOCATIONS

New York, NY (HQ)
Atlanta, GA • Boston, MA •
Chicago, IL • Dallas, TX •
Greenville, SC • Hartford, CT • Los
Angeles, CA • Miami, FL •
Minneapolis, MN • Morristown, NJ
• Orlando, FL • Pittsburgh, PA •
Sacramento, CA • San Francisco,
CA • Seattle, WA • Stamford, CT •
Vienna, VA • White Plains, NY •
Woodbury, NY •

THE STATS

No. of attorneys firm-wide: 369
No. of attorneys in New York: 37
No. of offices: 20
**Summer associate offers in New
York:** 2 out of 4 (2003)
Managing Partner: William A.
Krupman

UPPERS

- Employment law expertise
- Relaxed environment

DOWNERS

- Low pay
- Lame bonus structure

NOTABLE PERKS

- Flexible spending program
- Bar expenses
- Pre-tax transportation plan

MAJOR DEPARTMENTS & PRACTICES

Affirmative Action
Employee Benefits
Employment Litigation
Immigration
Labor Relations
Management Education
Workplace Safety
Workplace Substance Abuse

EMPLOYMENT CONTACT

Ms. Terry Clifford
Director of Human Resources
Phone: (914) 328-0404
Fax: (914) 328-9096
E-mail: recruiting@jacksonlewis.com

THE SCOOP

Founded in 1958, Jackson Lewis now has approximately 370 attorneys in 20 offices across the U.S. The firm exclusively represents employers in labor and employment issues, including litigation, immigration, affirmative action policy, management education and labor negotiations. In May 2002, the firm established the Jackson Lewis Scholarship Fund at the University of Michigan Law School to finance the legal education of students, especially minority students with interest in workplace law.

In addition to its Manhattan location, Jackson Lewis also works out of the nearby towns of White Plains and Woodbury. Two attorneys from the Woodbury office represented Minolta Business Solutions in a lawsuit brought by two former service technicians accusing the company of violating the federal Fair Labor Standards Act, as well as state laws pertaining to unpaid overtime work.

In October 2002, the district court judge presiding over the case denied a request by the plaintiffs for permission to invite other potential claimants to join them in the lawsuit. The decision runs counter to typical FLSA cases, in which claims that plaintiffs are similarly situated to other employees are usually granted with a very low threshold for evidence. Minolta thus benefited greatly from the decision, as it not only ended the prospect of a federal class-action lawsuit (barring further evidence) but made efforts to initiate a class action under the state laws more difficult as well.

GETTING HIRED

Check out Jackson Lewis' web site, www.jacksonlewis.com, for information about the firm's summer associate program. The web site also gives a brief description of the qualifications they are looking for in their hiring candidates.

Potential summer and full-time associates are encouraged to contact individual offices to pursue employment opportunities.

OUR SURVEY SAYS

For the most part, the associates at Jackson Lewis appear to be a fairly content bunch of lawyers. Insiders lavish praise on the "friendly, smart, fun [and] irreverent" atmosphere at the firm. One associate gushes, "Jackson Lewis has an incredibly friendly culture where lawyers have been with the firm for many years and [there is] relatively low turnover."

Other associates call Jackson Lewis "a conservative firm with fun people." Social butterflies will be happy at the firm. Says one insider, "The associates often socialize together, and generally there is a friendly and approachable atmosphere."

The praise of our sources extends beyond the associate classes to the firm partnership, too, and the friendly, happy feeling at the firm percolates from the top down. "To a person," reports one Jackson Lewis source, "the partners are unfailingly generous with their knowledge and good-natured in imparting it."

That doesn't mean associates love their bosses unconditionally. Some sources suggest discontentedly that it "wouldn't kill them to pay a better wage and bonus." One lawyer at the firm complains bluntly, "Jackson Lewis is below market on salary for a firm its size and does not have a good bonus structure." Still, this source (and others) is able to find the cloud's silver lining, admitting that the firm "is extremely flexible with personal/vacation time."

Jones Day

222 East 41st Street
New York, NY 10017-6702
Phone: (212) 326-3939
www.jonesday.com

LOCATIONS

Atlanta, GA • Chicago, IL •
Cleveland, OH • Columbus, OH •
Dallas, TX • Houston, TX • Irvine,
CA • Los Angeles, CA • Menlo
Park, CA • New York, NY •
Pittsburgh, PA • San Francisco, CA
• Washington, DC • Beijing •
Brussels • Frankfurt • Hong Kong •
London • Madrid • Milan •
Mumbai* • Munich • New Delhi* •
Paris • Shanghai • Singapore •
Sydney • Taipei • Tokyo

*P&A Law Offices, An Associate
Firm*

THE STATS

No. of attorneys firm-wide:
2,000+
No. of attorneys in New York: 219
No. of offices: 29
Summer associate offers firm-wide:
198 out of 224 (2003)
**Summer associate offers in New
York:** 33 out of 34 (2003)
Partner-in-Charge: Dennis W.
LaBarre
Hiring Partner: Jane Rue Wittstein

UPPERS

- Collegial co-workers, pleasant
  environment
- Solid training opportunities

DOWNERS

- Inconsistent
  mentoring/communication between
  partners and associates
- Below-par bonuses in New York

NOTABLE PERKS

- Moving expenses, plus movers who
  do the packing
- Twelve weeks maternity leave
- Annual retreats
- $4,000 stipend and $6,000
  interest-free loan

MAJOR DEPARTMENTS & PRACTICES

Bankruptcy
Capital Markets
General Litigation
Intellectual Property
Issues & Appeals
Lending/Structured Finance
Mergers & Acquisitions
Real Estate
Tax (including Employee Benefits)

EMPLOYMENT CONTACT

Ms. Shari J. Friedman
Recruiting Manager
Phone: (212) 326-3949
Fax: (212) 755-7306
E-mail: sfriedman@jonesday.com

BASE SALARY

New York, NY
1st year: $125,000
Summer associate: $10,400/month

THE SCOOP

When it comes to worldwide reach, few firms can match Jones Day's 2,000 lawyers in 29 offices around the globe. After nearly three decades as Jones, Day, Reavis & Pogue, the 110-year-old firm officially shortened its name to Jones Day in early 2003.

In a boon to the firm's international prestige, Jones Day scored a hat trick at the Asian Legal Business Awards in 2003 where awards won included "Managing Partner of the Year," "North American Law Firm of the Year" and "International Law Firm of the Year." The accolades don't stop there. *The American Lawyer* named Jones' Day's practice "Litigation Department of the Year." The firm's M&A practice consistently ranks No. 1 for number of deals worldwide according to Thomson Financial. The New York office won *Project Finance Magazine*'s "Deal of the Year" award in 2003 and won *Real Estate Investment and Finance* "Deal of the Year" as well for a transaction that was at the time the most expensive single asset real estate transaction in U.S. history.

Jones Day was tapped to argue on behalf of the state of Nevada in a lawsuit filed by a former employee who claims the state violated the Family and Medical Leave Act. New York-based associate Traci Lovitt acted as lead outside counsel for Nevada. As most of the legal industry's appellate litigators are based in Washington, this high profile case was a first step by Jones Day to build a strong appellate practice in New York.

GETTING HIRED

Although "Jones Day is not a school snob," many agree the firm looks harder at top-tier schools to fill its ranks. "Candidates generally must be from a first- or second-tier law school, although candidates at the top of their class from third- and even fourth-tier law schools will be considered," says one source. "Grades are given a lot of weight (rarely will someone who is not at least top third be considered), but people who have special talents or accomplishments who are under the grade cutoff are considered." Some New Yorkers think the firm should stick up for itself. "I think that our office has an inferiority complex vis-à-vis other New York law firms and as a consequence [we] sometimes sell ourselves a bit short in the interviewing process in terms of the credentials of candidates we consider," reports one lawyer.

OUR SURVEY SAYS

"Jones Day continues to be an oasis among law firms in New York," says one insider. "The work is sophisticated and challenging, the hours manageable and the environment pleasant. When I get up each day, I actually look forward to going to work – not something many senior associates can say – mainly because of the people." Partner/associate relations are sometimes strained, however. "[This] obviously depends on the partner, but many are vague, rushed and difficult to work with," says a source. "I've had some great experiences, but there are a few bad eggs out there," reports another associate.

"Although Jones Day pays market level annual salaries, the firm lags behind other large New York City firms in terms of bonuses," says one associate. "In addition, the firm strongly discourages us from discussing salary, even amongst ourselves." "Compensation is not lock-step," says another contact. "It is based on a combination of hours, efficiency and merit. Compensation for those at the top of the class is at, if not slightly above, market. However, in some years the firm has grudgingly paid market which makes the compensation bittersweet. In addition, bonuses, although generous, have not always matched the levels seen at other New York firms."

Associates aren't griping about the hours too much. True, some agree "they may have dropped the last two names, but it's still Jones, Day, Nights & Weekends." Most, though, find the hours at least on par with other New York firms. "The hours are completely manageable," says one attorney. "People work hard when necessary but there is also an appreciation that you need to be able to enjoy your life outside the firm, whether it is honoring a vacation, family engagement, birthday or just dinner plans."

"Jones Day is very conscious of training needs and has great programs," says one contact. "A lot of time and money is spent on very efficient, interesting training programs." That sentiment is shared by another insider: "The firm offers more in-house training opportunities than any other firm of which I am aware. The only drawback is that training outside the firm is not strongly encouraged."

Katten Muchin Zavis Rosenman

575 Madison Avenue
New York, NY 10022-2585
Phone: (212) 940-8800
www.kmzr.com

LOCATIONS

Chicago, IL (HQ)
Charlotte, NC
Los Angeles, CA
Newark, NJ
New York, NY
Palo Alto, CA
Washington, DC

THE STATS

No. of attorneys firm-wide: 600+
No. of attorneys in New York: 193
No. of offices: 7
Summer associate offers in New York: 13 out of 15 (2003)
National Managing Partner: Vincent A.F. Sergi
Hiring Partner: Jill D. Block (NY)

UPPERS

- Manageable hours
- Laid-back culture

DOWNERS

- Work assignment system often dysfunctional
- Unpopular deferred compensation system

NOTABLE PERKS

- One-month sabbatical after five years of service
- Free coffee, bagels and soft drinks
- Discounted legal expenses, including home closing costs
- Subsidized cafeteria

MAJOR DEPARTMENTS & PRACTICES

Customs & International Trade
Entertainment
Environment
Estate Planning
Financial Services
GeneralCorporate
Health Care
Intellectual Property
Litigation
Matrimonial
Real Estate
Sports Law & Sports Facilities
Structured Finance
Tax

EMPLOYMENT CONTACT

Ms. Kim McHugh
Legal Recruiting Manager
Phone: (212) 940-6386
E-mail: kim.mchugh@kmzr.com

BASE SALARY

New York, NY
1st year: $125,000
2nd year: $130,000
3rd year: $142,000
4th year: $157,000
5th year: $170,000
6th year: $180,000
7th year: $190,000
Summer associate: $2,403/week

THE SCOOP

Katten Muchin Zavis Rosenman was formed by the March 2002 merger of New York-based Rosenman & Colin and Chicago-based Katten Muchin Zavis. The new KMZ Rosenman is a respected technology, corporate and entertainment firm with over 600 lawyers in seven U.S. offices and clients such as Disney, Miramax, Showtime and Simpsons creator Matt Groening. KMZR is also known for its pro bono commitment, and was the first firm in Illinois to hire a partner dedicated to pro bono work.

KMZ Rosenman was involved in one of the largest deals of 2003 when it was tapped to represent NBC in the broadcast giant's merger with Vivendi Universal. Los Angeles-based partner Rik Toulon led the firm's team for the NBC deal, which included attorneys from the New York and Washington, D.C., offices.

The firm is representing brokerage house Heights Partners and one of its brokers in a sexual harassment suit filed by a trader on the American Stock Exchange. The plaintiff, an employee of one of Heights Partners' competitors, alleges that staff of the Heights Partners made unwelcome sexual advances and crude comments beginning in March 2000. The plaintiff complained to the Amex but claims the exchange failed to investigate and take action in a timely manner. The suit is pending.

GETTING HIRED

Recent economic conditions have allowed the firm to attract more candidates with top grades from top schools. "This firm seems to be about fit," says one source. "I think it goes without saying that they are looking for good work-product, but good people skills and a friendly nature seems to also be a focus. Usually on a call-back interview, the interviewee will meet with a combination of partners and associates. The firm also tries to accommodate having an interviewee interviewed by an attorney in an area of expressed interest, so both can get a sense of each other." Another associate says, "KMZ Rosenman, along with other large New York firms, has become increasingly selective as the economy has become worse. Several years ago, we were taking law students and laterals from anywhere. Now, even very promising and experienced laterals from top firms are being turned away."

OUR SURVEY SAYS

"I would describe the culture as laid-back and friendly," says one KMZ Rosenman insider. "Partners are always available to answer questions and help each other out in a crunch." Like many firms, culture can vary by department. "The firm culture has historically not been cohesive," says one lawyer who adds, "That is not a bad thing. It just means within the corporate department, at least in the New York office, the dynamic is defined by individual relationships between partners and associates, or between associates." This source, a former Rosenman & Colin employee, continues, "After our merger with KMZ, there has been a slight solidification of firm culture. But since the people in New York are the same, the dynamic is the same." The work assignment system has issues. "There is a lack of coordination when it comes to handing out assignments," complains one lawyer. "When work comes in, partners generally call the associates they know rather than going through the partners responsible for distributing work."

"The firm's expectations are very reasonable," says one source. "The nature of the practice – in terms of deal flow and client demands – can require long hours at times." New York holdovers from the pre-merger era notice a difference. "I billed 2,100 hours last year," says one attorney. "I consider myself lucky to have had the work, but there were times when intense periods disrupted family or other matters. This comes with being a lawyer at a large firm, of course. However, 2,100 hours was considered strong under legacy Rosenman, so it felt more worthwhile. Now that required hours are 2,000 and hours-based bonuses have been changed I don't feel as much of an incentive to bill more than the requirement, other than partnership considerations."

An associate reports, "My compensation is adequate, although I don't appreciate the lack of a truly clear pay scale for associates." Another source fumes, "The compensation structure is confusing and not at all as advertised. What they refer to as 'deferred comp' is actually a bonus based on hours billed." Yet another chimes in, "The firm has deferred compensation and therefore is not at market rate because barely anyone made their hours."

Kaye Scholer LLP

425 Park Avenue
New York, NY 10022-3598
Phone: (212) 836-8000
www.kayescholer.com

LOCATIONS

New York, NY (HQ)
Chicago, IL
Los Angeles, CA
Washington, DC
West Palm Beach, FL
Frankfurt
Hong Kong
London
Shanghai

THE STATS

No. of attorneys firm-wide: 475
No. of attorneys in New York: 350
No. of offices: 9
Summer associate offers firm-wide:
41 out of 41 (2003)
Summer associate offers in New
York: 31 out of 31 (2003)
Chairman: David Klingsberg
Managing Partner: Barry Willner
Hiring Partner: James Herschlein

UPPERS

• Top-notch antitrust practice
• Outstanding commitment to pro bono work

DOWNERS

• Deferred compensation system rankles
• Unpredictable hours

NOTABLE PERKS

• Yearly party at Central Park Zoo
• Technology subsidy (60 percent of cost of laptop)
• Friday cocktail hour
• Web-based meal ordering system

MAJOR DEPARTMENTS & PRACTICES

Antitrust
Business Reorganization
Corporate & Finance
Employment & Labor
Entertainment, Media &
  Communications
Intellectual Property
International
Legislative & Regulatory
Litigation
Product Liability
Real Estate
Tax
Technology & E-Commerce
Trust & Estates
White Collar Crime
Wills & Estates

EMPLOYMENT CONTACT

Ms. Wendy Evans
Director of Legal Personnel
Phone: (212) 836-8000
Fax: (212) 836-8689
E-mail: wevans@kayescholer.com

BASE SALARY

New York, NY
1st year: $125,000
2nd year: $135,000
3rd year: $150,000
4th year: $165,000
5th year: $186,000
6th year: $196,000
7th year: $205,000
8th year: $210,000
Summer associate: $2,410/week

THE SCOOP

A top-notch antitrust practice is the jewel in the crown of New York-based Kaye Scholer LLP. The firm, which has 475 lawyers in nine offices around the globe, also handles a wide variety of high-profile transactional work and has respected practices in bankruptcy, product liability, intellectual property and commercial litigation.

Founded way back in 1917 by a tax attorney/Broadway playwright, Kaye Scholer established one of the first labor practices in 1947. A few years later, the firm's star antitrust group was born, with Milton Handler at the helm. One of the firm's first antitrust victories was its successful challenge on behalf of Pepsi of Coca-Cola's exclusive use of the word "cola."

Kaye Scholer's litigation team continues to rack up victories. In June 2003, the firm successfully settled a lawsuit for elderly and disabled residents of the Neponsit Healthcare Facility in New York. Kaye Scholer won a victory for client Pfizer in March 2003 in a patent infringement dispute with the University of Rochester. Also in March 2003, a federal court dismissed a class-action lawsuit filed against Sallie Mae, a company that provides financial aid to college students and their families, by borrowers alleging unfair fees and interest.

GETTING HIRED

Insiders say the interview process at Kaye Scholer is "mostly about fit with the firm and personality." "Since recruiting standards are high," says a first-year, "it is assumed you can do the work. The issue then becomes one of fitting in with the culture of the firm and whether working with the candidate 60-plus hours a week would drive you nuts." "The interview process is a good one," observes one contact. "The focus in callbacks tends to be on the fit of the candidate within the firm culture, as his or her personality emerges through the interview process."

According to a litigator, "At the call-back stage, the offer is the candidate's to lose. No one looks at grades at this point, just personality." "The firm is focused on the ivy for summer hiring but looks to experience over law school pedigree in the lateral market," a senior associate reveals.

© 2004 Vault Inc.

OUR SURVEY SAYS

Most insiders praise Kaye Scholer's laid-back culture. "From the Camp Kaye summer associate program to Friday night cocktailing, the firm has tried to institutionalize socializing among attorneys and a more relaxed atmosphere than at some other large firms. I have noticed, though, over the years that attendance at the cocktail parties has waned some." "I chose Kaye because of its reputation as a more relaxed and less intense place than other New York firms, and so far the reputation has proved mostly true," says one attorney.

Kaye Scholer insiders are delighted with their firm's commitment to pro bono work, calling the firm "supportive," "encouraging" and "extremely committed." Sources appreciate that "pro bono hours are counted the same as billable hours for bonus purposes," which they say is a strong sign of the firm's committment. Says one third-year, "Can't ask for more."

Kaye Scholer "is traditionally known for being on the cheaper side of the firm spectrum" and "doesn't give more than it has to." But it does "keep up to par" with the competition and is "competitive with regard to the year-end bonus." Although one insider chirps, "I have absolutely no complaints about my salary," many others voice concern over the firm's "unpopular" deferred compensation system. Complains one attorney, "The 15 percent deferred compensation – the firm takes out 15 percent of your pay and gives it back to you at the end of January of the next year – is a pain in the neck, antiquated, paternalistic and not disclosed to applicants unless they ask."

Associates are less peeved when it comes to their hours, though they echo the familiar complaints of countless big-firm associates before them. "The problem with our hours is that they are completely unpredictable," gripes one associate. "I feel either underused or overused. Your work hours also vary wildly depending on who you work for. [But] the people I've worked for have been overall considerate and ask us to stay late only if necessary for the work." "Kaye Scholer is no worse than other firms and is perhaps better than some," says one litigator. "That being said, the hours expected from attorneys in New York have gotten out of hand. I get up, go to work, go home, go to bed. Then I repeat it the next day."

Most Kaye Scholer associates are pleased with their bosses, reporting that "on the whole, the good partners outnumber the bad." Reveals one senior litigator, "My personal experience with the partners here has been fantastic, and I have heard very few, if any, horror stories." And one first-year insists, "So far, the two times I have seen partners lose their temper – once with me, and once with a colleague – they have apologized shortly thereafter."

Kelley Drye & Warren LLP

101 Park Avenue
New York, NY 10178-0002
Phone (212) 808-7800
www.kelleydrye.com

LOCATIONS

New York, NY (HQ)
Chicago, IL
Parsippany, NJ
Stamford, CT
Tysons Corner, VA
Washington, DC
Brussels

THE STATS

No. of attorneys firm-wide: 325
No. of attorneys in New York: 200
No. of offices: 7
Summer associate offers firm-wide:
24 out of 27 (2003)
Summer associate offers in New York: 19 out of 21 (2003)
Chairman: John M. Callagy
Hiring Partner: Gregory M. McKenzie

UPPERS

- Great partner/associate relations
- Reasonable hours

DOWNERS

- Training tough to come by
- Skimping on bonuses

NOTABLE PERKS

- BlackBerry pagers
- Monthly cocktail parties and lunches
- Bar expenses in multiple jurisdictions
- Real estate attorney to handle home purchases

MAJOR DEPARTMENTS & PRACTICES

Bankruptcy
Corporate
Employee Benefits
Environmental
Labor/Employment
Litigation
Private Clients
Real Estate
Tax
Telecommunications

EMPLOYMENT CONTACT

Mr. Randy Liss
Recruiting Coordinator
Phone: (212) 808-7721
Fax: (212) 808-7897
E-mail: rliss@kelleydrye.com

BASE SALARY

New York, NY
1st year: $125,000
2nd year: $135,000
3rd year: $150,000
4th year: $165,000
5th year: $180,000
6th year: $195,000
7th year: $205,000
Summer associate: $2,403.85/week

THE SCOOP

Kelley Drye & Warren has been around the block. Founded in 1836, the firm is one of the oldest law practitioners in the United States and even boasts then-President Abraham Lincoln as a former client. Kelley Drye now has approximately 325 lawyers in seven offices in the United States and Europe, plus four affiliate offices in Asia. The firm is known for its bankruptcy, tax, telecommunications and litigation work.

In August 2002, Kelly Drye welcomed James S. Gilmore III, the former governor of Virginia and chairman of the Republican National Committee, as a partner in the firm's Washington, D.C., office. Gilmore took on lobbying and corporate work for the firm. In March 2003, Kelley Drye closed its Los Angeles office due to disappointing revenue.

In early 2003, Kelley Drye successfully represented long-time client JPMorgan Chase in an Enron-related action. The super-bank settled a dispute with 11 insurance companies regarding complex transactions JPMorgan had with the bankrupted energy trader. JPMorgan filed a $1.1 billion lawsuit against the insurance companies, claiming they refused to cover the company's losses in several failed energy trades that took place in the late 1990s. The insurers claimed the deals in question were among the accounting tricks that eventually brought Enron down.

GETTING HIRED

Kelley Drye associates agree that when it comes to hiring, "pedigree isn't too important." What is important? "People skills," says one insider, "probably because there's an underlying soft spot for litigation skills and talk-ability." Others agree: being nice is important. "I don't think stellar academic credentials matter as much as being the kind of person people want to work with," says one source. "Our firm requires excellent credentials as well as a good personality fit," reports one lawyer.

Insiders believe the firm is selective when choosing new associates – but not overly so. "In a good economy, [getting hired] was easy, but it has been much more competitive recently," says one associate. Indeed, one veteran Kelley Drye lawyer muses, "I wonder whether I'd get hired today."

OUR SURVEY SAYS

Overall, Kelley Drye associates are pleased with life at their firm. "Kelley Drye has been a great place to work," remarks one associate. "I believe it is a meritocracy. The partners assign work based on your performance. [This is a] great place for people who are interested in learning and working hard." Informality abounds. "The atmosphere is informal, mostly because most of the lawyers don't take themselves too seriously," says one attorney. "Kelley Drye is in general a laid-back place to work, but when a big case comes along everyone takes it very seriously and really steps up," says one source.

Firm associates are generally satisfied with their hours, but they do worry about hitting their billable target. "We really do have a 2,000-hour target," reports one source. "People who do not hit the target are not punished or fired. They simply do not get a bonus." Some departments are scrambling for work. "In litigation, the hours rat race is on," says one attorney from that department. "People are always comparing billables and making sure they have more than the next guy. The smaller groups are not like that, but that is also because there is generally less work. People in the smaller groups come in, bill their six to eight hours and go home." Associates' lives have been made easier by technology. "With BlackBerrys made available and a good dial-in service, I'm able to work as well from home as from inside the office, meaning I can get my work done as needed from where needed and not lose a step."

Bonus time isn't always a happy time at Kelley Drye. "I have no complaints about my base salary," says one senior associate. "I appreciate getting paid over $200,000 per year. The bonus policy at the firm, however, is completely arbitrary." "We keep up with other firms in terms of general salary, but bonuses are abysmal," growls one contact. "The firm no longer even maintains a pretense of competing with other firms in terms of bonuses." The timing of the bonus checks could be better. Reports one associate, "The bonus is perhaps a little below market value and is paid later than at other firms – end of February this year. That said, we are extremely well paid."

Kenyon & Kenyon

One Broadway
New York, NY 10004-1050
Phone: (212) 425-7200
www.kenyon.com

LOCATIONS

New York, NY (HQ)
San Jose, CA
Washington, DC

THE STATS

No. of attorneys firm-wide: 206
No. of attorneys in New York: 142
No. of offices: 3
Summer associate offers firm-wide:
22 out of 24 (2003)
**Summer associate offers in New
York:** 18 out of 19 (2003)
Managing Partner: Robert T. Tobin
Hiring Partner: Walter E. Hanley Jr.

UPPERS

- Laid-back, friendly culture
- Reasonable hours; no face time

DOWNERS

- Sink-or-swim training
- Questionable commitment to diversity

NOTABLE PERKS

- Yearly black-tie dinner
- Discounted gym membership
- Emergency child care

MAJOR DEPARTMENTS & PRACTICES

Counseling
Licensing
Patent Litigation & Prosecution
Trademark Litigation & Prosecution
Technologies: Internet &
Information
  Technology
Technologies: Life Sciences
Technologies: Mechanical/Product
  Design

EMPLOYMENT CONTACT

Ms. Kathleen Lynn
Director of Recruiting
Phone: (212) 908-6177
Fax: (212) 425-5288
E-mail: klynn@kenyon.com

BASE SALARY

New York, NY
1st year: $125,000
2nd year: $135,000
3rd year: $145,000
4th year: $160,000
5th year: $180,000
6th year: $190,000
7th year: $200,000
8th year: $210,000

THE SCOOP

For IP and patent expertise, double your pleasure at Kenyon & Kenyon, a 200-lawyer firm based in New York with offices in San Jose, Calif., and Washington, D.C. The 125-year old firm is involved in all kinds of intellectual property law including litigation, patents, trademarks and copyrights, and transactions.

If you know what a mass spectrometer system is, Kenyon & Kenyon might be the firm for you. In 2002, Kenyon successfully represented client Applera Corp. in a patent case that was listed in the *National Law Journal*'s biggest verdicts of 2002. Kenyon lawyers defended its client's patent of, yes, a mass spectrometer system. The court found the patent to be valid and infringed by the defendant and awarded lost profits of $47.5 million.

In another recent case that helped define the limits of fraudulent trademark applications, Kenyon & Kenyon won a victory for Medinol, a medical device manufacturer base in Tel Aviv, Israel. Medinol took issue with a trademark registration filed by Maple Grove, Minn.-based Neuro Vasx in August 2000. Neuro Vasx wanted to trademark the name Nirovascular for use in connection with stents the company manufacturers. Medinol challenged the application, saying that Neuro Vasx committed fraud because it never used the name Nirovascular for its stents; Neuro Vasx claimed the error was the result of an oversight and tried to amend the patent. In May 2003, the U.S. Patent and Trademark Office sided with Medinol, saying that Neuro Vasx's application was fraudulent even if the company's mistake was unintentional.

GETTING HIRED

Kenyon & Kenyon seeks 20-25 summer associates each year and, because of its IP focus, values science backgrounds. The firm's web site, www.kenyon.com, lists the details of its summer associate program. Each associate is assigned a mentor and a buddy to get them through the Kenyon summer experience. Also, the firm sponsors a number of seminars, lunches and other events to introduce summer associates to the firm and to each other. Kenyon & Kenyon's web site also lists open lateral positions and pertinent contact information.

OUR SURVEY SAYS

Associates say the Kenyon & Kenyon vibe is "generally laid-back and friendly." The firm has "no screamers. Good work is expected, but partners are fairly forgiving." According to sources, there are "no barriers to interacting with any partner." Those looking to join the Kenyon partnership should know the firm recently made changes to its partnership track. "Recently the partnership track was changed from eight years to some yet-to-be-defined term, and we now have a non-equity track," says an insider.

At Kenyon, as at other top firms, expect "a lot of work if you want to succeed." "When you have work to do, you are expected to get it done," says a source. "However face time is not important." The firm's pay structure is on par with the industry as well. "[Pay] is average for New York City," notes an attorney. "However, from what I hear from friends at other firms, the bonuses at Kenyon are a bit lower than at other firms." (Kenyon points out that for fiscal year 2003, bonuses ranged from $5,000 to $103,000, depending on quality of work, seniority and hours.)

Kenyon insiders say there's room for improvement when it comes to training. "We receive no training," gripes a midlevel associate. "We are expected to check the document management system for a similar document – i.e., a preliminary injunction brief – and tailor ours in that fashion. There is little or no guidance." "It's all hands on," agrees another contact. "There is no formal training." Be ready to get burned. "You're thrown into the fire, and you should figure out how to survive on your own," warns an associate.

Insiders also question the firm's commitment to diversity. Observes one source, "If you want a family, wait until after you make partner. Otherwise you will go through hell trying to balance family and work life. In fact, I think women who switch to part time to stay home for a while with the kids are treated like second-class citizens." "Women are not given the respect that men are, regardless of the quality of work," complains a source. Others notice that Kenyon & Kenyon "seems to have some trouble retaining minority associates, but [it's] not clear if this is any fault of the firm."

Kirkland & Ellis

Citigroup Center
153 East 53rd Street
New York, NY 10022-4611
Phone: (212) 446-4800
www.kirkland.com

LOCATIONS

Chicago, IL (HQ)
Los Angeles, CA
New York, NY
San Francisco, CA
Washington, DC
London

THE STATS

No. of attorneys firm-wide: 913
No. of attorneys in New York: 190
No. of offices: 6
Summer associate offers firm-wide:
115 out of 117 (2003)
**Summer associate offers in New
York:** 20 out of 20 (2003)
Firm Administrator: Douglas O.
McLemore
Hiring Partner: Jonathan Putnam

UPPERS

- Great training and early
  responsibility
- Big-league prestige

DOWNERS

- Mysterious bonus system leads to
  associate angst
- Lackluster commitment to pro bono
  work

NOTABLE PERKS

- $10,000 summer stipend for pre-
  first year summer
- $300 art budget for office
  decoration
- Money for outside CLE courses
- Free fruit and bagels every morning

MAJOR DEPARTMENTS & PRACTICES

Bankruptcy
Intellectual Property
Litigation
Tax & Planning
Transactional

EMPLOYMENT CONTACT

Ms. Susan E. Elitzky
Attorney Recruiting Manager
Phone: (212) 446-4680
Fax: (212) 446-4900
E-mail: selitzky@kirkland.com

BASE SALARY

New York, NY
1st year: $125,000
2nd year: $135,000
3rd year: $150,000
4th year: $170,000
5th year: $190,000
6th year: $205,000
Summer associate: $2,404/week

THE SCOOP

Founded in 1908 by two Chicago lawyers, Kirkland & Ellis boasts respected litigation, bankruptcy, intellectual property, tax, antitrust, M&A and private equity practices. The firm has over 900 attorneys in six offices, and its New York outpost, founded in 1990, now has 175 lawyers. One of the firm's best known attorneys is Kenneth Starr, the Whitewater special prosecutor whose investigation led to the impeachment of President Bill Clinton. Among his current cases is a challenge to the McCain-Feingold campaign finance law.

K&E is used to getting awards. *The National Law Journal* included two of the firm's litigation victories (for clients General Motors and Kubota Corp.) in its list of the Top Defense Wins of the Year for 2002. The *Corporate Counsel* survey of Fortune 250 companies recently ranked K&E as the single most used firm by the nation's largest corporations for both litigation and IP. K&E was ranked No. 5 by AmLaw in profits per partner in 2003, the only non-New York-based firm in the top 15, and was one of five finalists for Litigation Department of the Year in 2003. Moreover, U.K. legal publisher Chambers & Partners called K&E Private Equity International Firm of the Year in 2002 and U.S. Private Equity Firm of the Year in 2003.

K&E avoided ignominy in 2002 when a federal judge dismissed claims against the firm in a class-action suit filed by Enron shareholders. A federal judge agreed with K&E's argument that since it was not involved in the fallen energy giant's alleged malfeasance, the firm was not liable for the massive losses to investors.

GETTING HIRED

K&E can afford to be picky. It "only hires the smartest candidates from the best law schools," say our sources. The firm "selects people based on skill, motivation and ability to work well with others in the firm" and "is looking for self-starters, people with determination to do well who don't wait to be spoon-fed." A "down-to-earth personality is very important," and "you don't get anywhere in the firm by being rude." It helps to have the "eye of the tiger." "The firm is looking for new associates with top grades, top schools and a little something extra – a heart or fire in their bellies," says an associate, who adds the firm is seeking "someone who is not afraid to work."

OUR SURVEYS SAYS

Kirkland & Ellis is "friendly but very intense, and very oriented toward pushing the idea that we're the best and should always work toward being the best," says one contact. "Kirkland has a camaraderie that is contagious," reports a midlevel associate. "You are surrounded by talented, challenging, energetic colleagues who are working toward the same goals as you are."

"The Kirkland trade-off is clear – with great work and great responsibility comes a request for greater commitment," says one insider. "If you are efficient and are good about working at home, you can strike an excellent balance, but the responsibility for doing so rests with the individual." Another source muses, "On the one hand, I love the fact that the firm entrusts me with a lot of responsibility and opportunity. On the other hand, having all those responsibilities and opportunities translates into a lot of hours. But as I see it, no true, aspiring trial lawyer could expect to have one without the other, and in any event the firm does not hound people to put in hours for the sake of hours alone. Getting the job done and done well are the only motivations."

Although "base salaries are pretty well known," sources admit "the bonus grid is a secret." "How many hours is the quota for various bonuses? No one knows or no one will tell. What is the dollar amount of bonuses at any given level? That's a secret. How was my bonus determined? Not telling." Bonus disgruntlement abounds. "I expected to work hard at Kirkland but not to be paid bonuses below market," complains a source. The firm points out that the bonus system is a meritocracy based on level of performance and that many associates receive bonuses significantly above the market level.

Litigators lusting for superb training opportunities should look no further than Kirkland and its famous "Kirkland Institute of Trial Advocacy" [KITA] program. "The reason I decided to come here [is] the training that the firm invests in its associates, both through its own extensive KITA program and through the great opportunities you can get on various cases," says one litigator. "Plus, consistent with its intense approach to litigating, the partners here all seem to take pride in teaching its younger ranks, either via a formal training program or when you work directly with them on a case."

Associates are less effusive when it comes to pro bono. Sources bemoan the fact that there is no pro bono committee, and some wish the firm would be more supportive. "The onus is on the associate to find the project they want to work on," explains one insider, "to get the necessary approvals and to get a partner to support it."

Kramer Levin Naftalis & Frankel LLP

919 Third Avenue
New York, NY 10022-3852
Phone: (212) 715-9100
www.kramerlevin.com

LOCATIONS

New York, NY (HQ)
Paris

Affiliations with the Studio Santa Maria firm in Italy and an alliance with the UK-based Berwin Leighton Paisner

THE STATS

No. of attorneys firm-wide: 285
No. of attorneys in New York: 264
No. of offices: 2
Summer associate offers firm-wide: 16 out of 16 (2003)
Summer associate offers in New York: 16 out of 16 (2003)
Co-Chairmen: Thomas E. Constance, Ezra G. Levin, Gary P. Naftalis
Hiring Partner: Barry H. Berke

UPPERS

- Manageable hours
- Laid-back culture

DOWNERS

- Lack of socializing among attorneys
- Bonuses tied to billable hours

NOTABLE PERKS

- Business development budget for associates
- Bar expenses and bar membership dues
- Computer reimbursement program
- Percentage of fees received from clients brought into the firm

MAJOR DEPARTMENTS & PRACTICES

Antitrust
Appellate & Constitutional
Litigation
Banking
Corporate
Creditors' Rights & Bankruptcy
Employee Benefits
Employment & Labor
Environmental
False Advertising
Financial Services
Individual Client
Intellectual Property
International
Land Use
Litigation
Real Estate
Tax

EMPLOYMENT CONTACT

Ms. Pamela H. Nelson
Director of Legal Recruiting
Phone: (212) 715-9213
Fax: (212) 715-8000
E-mail: pnelson@kramerlevin.com

BASE SALARY

New York, NY
1st year: $125,000
Summer associate: $2,404/week

THE SCOOP

Founded in 1968, Kramer Levin Naftalis & Frankel LLP's 285 lawyers are split between offices in New York and Paris. The firm also has affiliations with Italian and U.K.-based firms, and its practice areas include corporate, employee benefits/ERISA and intellectual property.

In recent months, Kramer Levin's pro bono practice has won asylum cases for gay, HIV-positive men from Colombia and Egypt who claimed their sexual orientation and HIV status would subject them to persecution. Kramer Levin filed an amicus brief in the Lawrence v. Texas case. In June 2003 the Supreme Court stuck down a Texas law prohibiting consensual sex acts between same-sex partners on privacy grounds.

Kramer Levin went to the mat in July 2003 for client Star Boxing, a New York-based boxing promoter. Star filed a breach of contract complaint against Antonio "The Magic Man" Tarver. The claim, heard by an arbitrator, alleged that Tarver violated an exclusive promotional contract with Star Boxing by signing an agreement with another promoter. The arbitrator agreed with Star, banning Tarver from fighting for any other company and granting Star monetary damages. The firm also knocked tennis player Martina Hingis' multimillion-dollar lawsuit against Italian athletic shoemaker Sergio Tacchini out of the courts. Hingis blamed Tacchini's products for the foot injuries that cut her career short.

GETTING HIRED

Kramer Levin's recruiting process is pretty straightforward; the firm hits most of the big Eastern law schools including Harvard, Penn, Columbia and NYU, and Midwestern heavy hitters like Chicago and Michigan. Additionally, the firm recruits at regional powers like Cardozo, Brooklyn Law School and St. John's University. After the initial on-campus screening interview, candidates have a half-day of interviews at the firm's New York office that concludes with a lunch with two attorneys. Personality is a key issue. "I think the firm is generally looking to hire hardworking and friendly people," notes one attorney. Clerking experience is also helpful. "At least in the litigation department, this firm emphasizes hiring former law clerks," says a litigator.

OUR SURVEY SAYS

One insider describes Kramer Levin as "pretty laid-back, not a factory" and a place where they "expect that you will get your work done properly." "Lawyers are very friendly with one another, the firm culture is cordial and respectful," according to another source. Others agree that the firm is a nice place to work, though party animals may want to look elsewhere. "Unfortunately many lawyers do not tend to socialize together outside of work," mourns one litigator. "The litigation department is trying to have more social gatherings, and some associates go out, but that is it." The culture may have changed for the worse recently. One associate complains Kramer Levin "used to be [a] lifestyle [firm] – now it's a little big firm with the echoes of the lifestyle past." Partners are said to be "demanding, yet patient."

Long hours aren't a big problem at Kramer Levin. "The amount of hours worked is very manageable," reports one source. Another lawyer says the hours are "usually not so bad – rarely weekends." Be warned, though, that "when you get busy, you get very busy." The good part is "the hours are sometimes long, but people appreciate your hard work," notes a contact. One lawyer notices "the pressure to work longer hours is increasing."

"While the firm, at lower level, matches other big firms in the city, at higher levels it doesn't keep up. The bonus structure is also behind. Technically the firm's high bonus is the same as other firms, but to get to the high bonus you have to be a stellar associate working some 2,300 hours," a litigator gripes. Though one insider complains of "big-firm pay, but not big-firm perks," others point out that the firm pays bar expenses, bar membership dues and a bonus for bringing in new business.

"Training comes mostly through informal mentoring," observes a third-year, who adds, "The firm has recently begun instituting more formal training programs." "Training is by way of giving you more responsibility on either pro bono cases or smaller litigations," says a source. "While the firm has some in-house training programs, most of the training comes from hands-on experience on cases," agrees another contact. "Most cases are staffed 1:1, so there can be a significant opportunity for learning."

Kronish Lieb Weiner & Hellman LLP

1114 Avenue of the Americas
New York, NY 10036-7798
Phone: (212) 479-6000
www.klwh.com

LOCATIONS

New York, NY

THE STATS

No. of attorneys firm-wide: 110
No. of attorneys in New York: 110
No. of offices: 1
Summer associate offers: 8 out of 8 (2003)
Managing Partner: Alan Levine
Hiring Partner: Steven M. Cohen

UPPERS

- Close-knit culture
- Reasonable hours, little pressure to bill

DOWNERS

- Muddled policy for new-business bonus
- Sink-or-swim training

NOTABLE PERKS

- Firm-sponsored CLE and bar expenses
- Monthly cocktail parties
- Partially subsidized gym membership

MAJOR DEPARTMENTS & PRACTICES

Bankruptcy
Corporate & Commercial
Litigation
Real Estate
Taxation
Trusts & Estates

EMPLOYMENT CONTACT

Ms. Tina Antonakakis, Esq.
Dir. Legal Recruitment & Professional
Development
E-mail: legalrecruiting@kronishlieb.com

BASE SALARY

New York, NY
1st year: $125,000
Summer associate: $2,400/week

THE SCOOP

With over 100 lawyers in its sole office in New York, Kronish Lieb Weiner & Hellman caters to big companies. Financial institutions are one of the firm's specialties: its clients include commercial banks like Allied Irish Banks, HSBC and Dime Savings Bank; investment banks and brokerage houses like Credit Suisse First Boston and Cantor Fitzgerald; insurers like the Hartford Cos., St. Paul Fire and Marine Insurance, and Met Life; and accountants like KPMG and Ernst & Young. Kronish Lieb also has a very active white-collar crime practice and has played a role in high-profile cases involving ImClone, Martha Stewart and Goldman Sachs.

Kronish Lieb is one of the many law firms representing parties in the mother of all corporate scandals, the Enron fraud and bankruptcy. The firm has represented Enron's Employee Committee in its attempt to recover as much money as possible for employees of the disgraced energy company. In September 2003, a federal judge ruled in favor of the Employee Committee, allowing it to collect part of a $53 million pool set aside for deferred compensation for Enron executives.

In a recent victory for Kronish Lieb client KPMG, a special master recommended in October 2003 that the accounting firm should not be made to produce documents related to tax shelters the firm established for clients. The IRS, seeking the documents, claimed that confidentiality protections didn't apply to the records. The court agreed with Kronish Lieb's argument that the records were protected as confidential advice given to KPMG clients.

GETTING HIRED

The hiring process at Kronish Lieb is pretty laid-back, say our sources. Notes one insider, "At the callbacks, candidates will interview with four attorneys. These interviews are informal and hopefully fun. I had a great time when I interviewed for a summer associate position." The firm wants people who want Kronish Lieb. "The firm is looking for people who aren't so worried about working for the biggest law firm they can find and who want to stick around for a long time," says one insider. The right school is important. The firm "requires top-notch legal talents that are willing to embrace the steep learning curve. This generally translates into an implied recruiting motto: 'Students outside the top-20 law schools need not apply.'"

OUR SURVEY SAYS

Most associates agree that "the culture at Kronish Lieb is great. All of the attorneys are friendly and approachable and do tend to socialize together. There is no stuffiness." "The atmosphere is very friendly, not uptight at all," agrees a source. "The partners are very approachable." Some complain that, although "the firm is relatively laid-back and friendly," "the departments do not mix very much, so it is hard to get to know colleagues in other departments." One insider points out that the firm is "small enough that through firm receptions and just walking around you can meet every other lawyer and staff member."

Associates are generally satisfied with their compensation, especially considering the money/hours trade-off at Kronish Lieb. "Compensation, like at most New York firms, is outstanding," says one source. "I don't think the firm awards huge bonuses, but it is an acceptable trade-off for the good working conditions and hours." Some complain that senior associates are shortchanged. "The starting salary at Kronish Lieb for first-year associates is on par with all of the other top mid- to large-sized law firms in New York," says one attorney. "However, as associates reach the fifth- to ninth-year levels, the base salaries are approximately 20 percent lower than those offered by large law firms but may be competitive with mid-sized law firms." Associates also complain that, though Kronish Lieb has a 10 percent bonus for new business brought into the firm, the bonus is rarely paid out due to severe restrictions on what constitutes new business.

Kronish Lieb isn't putting undue pressures on its associates' schedules. "When Kronish Lieb is busy, people here bill time comparable to larger firms," says one insider. "But I would not say there is pressure to bill. You are expected to work as long as necessary to complete the work you've been assigned but not to put in face time." Another contact agrees, saying "There's no face time here – you're only here late when there's work to be done."

Those looking for in-depth training sessions may find themselves uncomfortable in the sink-or-swim atmosphere at Kronish, although some insiders thrive on the responsibility they receive from day one. "KLWH throws their young associates into the fire immediately, expecting the associates to seek out guidance rather than having the associates babysat," says one associate. Those who think the real-life experience they gain at their firm is more valuable than more formal training programs say, "You are much more likely to be thrown into a real-life deposition than go to a workshop on how to take a deposition."

Latham & Watkins LLP

885 Third Avenue
Suite 1000
New York, NY 10022-4802
Phone: (212) 906-1200
www.lw.com

LOCATIONS

Boston, MA • Chicago, IL • Costa
Mesa, CA • Los Angeles, CA •
Newark, NJ • New York, NY •
Reston, VA • San Diego, CA • San
Francisco, CA • Silicon Valley, CA
• Washington, DC • Brussels •
Frankfurt • Hamburg • Hong Kong
• London • Milan • Moscow • Paris
• Singapore • Tokyo

THE STATS

No. of attorneys firm-wide: 1,532
No. of attorneys in New York: 265
No. of offices: 21
Summer associate offers firm-wide:
142 out of 148 (2003)
**Summer associate offers in New
York:** 25 out of 26 (2003)
Chairman: Robert Dell
Hiring Partner: Tracy Edmonson

UPPERS

- High-profile litigation department
- "A+ training"

DOWNERS

- "Stingy" bonuses
- Billable hour target rankles

NOTABLE PERKS

- International office exchange program
- Annual weekend firm-wide meeting
- CLE reimbursement
- Soda for a quarter (not all locations)

MAJOR DEPARTMENTS & PRACTICES

Communications

Corporate

Environment, Land & Resources

Finance/Real Estate

Health Care

Insolvency

Litigation

M&A

Tax

Venture & Technology

EMPLOYMENT CONTACT

Ms. Maureen K. Fontana
Recruiting Manager
Phone: (212) 906-1200
E-mail: maureen.fontana@lw.com

BASE SALARY

New York, NY
1st year: $125,000
2nd year: $135,000
Summer associate: $2,400/week

THE SCOOP

The largest law firm in California, Latham & Watkins LLP has five offices in in the Golden State, but 21 overall, including 10 outside the United States. In June 2003, *The Lawyer*, a U.K.-based legal trade publication, named Latham & Watkins "U.S. Law Firm of the Year," citing Latham's rapid European buildup and lateral hires in capital markets and corporate finance.

Latham, along with Wilmer, Cutler & Pickering, defended the University of Michigan in a high-profile case before the U.S. Supreme Court involving the contentious issue of affirmative action. Partner Maureen Mahoney argued for Michigan's law school, defending its policy of awarding points to minority applicants. In June 2003, the Court upheld the policy. *The Daily Journal* awarded Mahoney the best individual oral argument for the 2003 Supreme Court term. Also in 2003, Latham successfully defended AutoZone in a $1 billion federal antitrust lawsuit in New York. Moreover, Latham's New York lawyers recently scored significant victories for Nintendo of America, two of which were related to the popular Pokemon characters.

Latham has made substantial advances in its pro bono practice over the past decade, when a 1994 survey ranked the firm in the bottom third of the nation's law firms when it came to pro bono hours. It now racks up awards for its public service work, including recognition by the American Bar Association with its 2003 Pro Bono Publico Award. According to *The American Lawyer*'s survey, Latham had the most pro bono hours of any U.S. firm last year.

GETTING HIRED

Latham expects "the whole package" in its hires but emphasizes academic stature above other qualities. "If you didn't go to the right law school and graduate in the right percentage of your class," warns one insider, "your chances are next to nil." Furthermore, another source relays, "the GPA requirements have been going up steadily as the economy has slowed." The "smart, driven, normal" associates at Latham survive a "rigorous" call-back process, interviewing with up to seven associates in a single day. "It is very important to Latham to keep a good firm culture," explains a litigation associate. Therefore, the firm looks to hire only "good-natured people." "If you're relaxed, have some fun and aren't cocky, chances are you'll do well," another insider shares.

OUR SURVEY SAYS

One associate describes Latham & Watkins as "a very friendly firm that pretty much has something for everyone." But it's "not a party place," cautions a junior litigator, who adds there's "not much socializing between the lawyers once you're past the second year." Other sources describe "a very strong frat boy culture" and warn of cliques within Latham. "Belonging to the 'in' crowd in a department is crucial to have work assigned to you," a midlevel corporate attorney laments. "Not always, but too often," a colleague agrees, "the good work is distributed on the basis of politics, not quality of work or merit."

Latham "manages to combine a laid-back attitude with enormous emphasis on hours," and "will push you as hard as you let them." But, a second-year reflects, "I do not think that Latham is a sweatshop and I have many friends at other firms who are much more disenchanted with the hours." A midlevel associate admits, "I work a little more than I would like, but about as much as I anticipated." Caseloads are somewhat lighter because of the economy, but that doesn't necessarily make associates feel more relaxed. "I was expecting to get here and have plenty of interesting work to do," complains a first-year, "and instead, sometimes I sit around and do nothing all day waiting for an assignment."

A midlevel associate describes the base salary as "fair," but calls the firm "stingy with bonuses." A first-year echoes the complaint that "bonuses have not necessarily been commensurate with firm earnings," while even a "more than satisfied" second-year has "a sense that bonuses this year were less generous than at some other firms." Another sophomore gripes, "The firm continues to make more money than ever, but bonuses are allocated right at market or below."

"In my time here," says one veteran corporate attorney, "Latham & Watkins has moved from adequate to top-notch in training. The firm made it a goal and now really emphasizes it." Today, the firm offers "the best and most comprehensive training program of any firm," with "more formal training sessions than any one person can attend." ("I'd almost describe the training as overkill," one third-year exclaims.) But, says a junior associate, "I've found the informal training and mentoring to be even more valuable."

LeBoeuf, Lamb, Green & MacRae, L.L.P.

125 West 55th Street
New York, NY 10019-5389
Phone: (212) 424-8000
www.llgm.com

LOCATIONS

New York, NY (HQ)
Albany, NY • Boston, MA •
Harrisburg, PA • Hartford, CT •
Houston, TX • Jacksonville, FL •
Los Angeles, CA • Newark, NJ •
Pittsburgh, PA • Salt Lake City, UT
• San Francisco, CA • Washington,
DC • Almaty, Kazakhstan • Beijing
• Bishkek, Kyrgyzstan • Brussels •
Johannesburg • London • Moscow
• Paris • Riyadh, Saudi Arabia •
Tashkent, Uzbekistan

THE STATS

No. of attorneys firm-wide: 650
No. of attorneys in New York: 233
No. of offices: 23
Summer associate offers firm-wide:
54 out of 56 (2003)
Summer associate offers in
NewYork: 30 out of 30 (2003)
Chairman: Steven H. Davis
Hiring Partner: William G. Primps

UPPERS

• Competitive salaries
• Manageable hours

DOWNERS

• Increased emphasis on billable hours
• So much insurance work can be
  tiresome

NOTABLE PERKS

• CLE and bar expenses paid
• Discounted gym memberships
• Moving expenses for first-years
• On-site dining room (in New York)

MAJOR DEPARTMENTS & PRACTICES

Bankruptcy & Restructuring
Corporate
Energy
Environmental, Health & Safety
Executive Compensation, Employee
 Benefits & ERISA
Insurance
International
Litigation
Real Estate
Reinsurance
Tax
Technology & Intellectual Property
Telecommunications
Trusts & Estates

EMPLOYMENT CONTACT

Ms. Jill Cameron
Manager of Legal Recruiting
Phone: (212) 424-8266
Fax: (212) 424-8500
E-mail: jcameron@llgm.com

BASE SALARY

New York, NY
1st year: $125,000
2nd year: $135,000
3rd year: $150,000
4th year: $170,000
5th year: $190,000
6th year: $200,000
7th year: $205,000
8th year: $210,000
Summer associate: $2,404/week

THE SCOOP

Founded in 1929, LeBoeuf, Lamb, Greene & MacRae, L.L.P. has built a multinational practice by focusing on three core industries: insurance, finance and energy. The firm has 650 lawyers in 13 locations in the U.S. and 10 overseas locations, including Moscow and cities in three other former Soviet republics.

LeBoeuf's reputation has been built, in part, by its work in the insurance industry. It was tops among U.S. law firms in nominations to Euromoney Legal Media Group's "Guide to the World's Leading Insurance and Reinsurance Lawyers" in November 2002. *Reaction* magazine named LeBoeuf "Reinsurance Law Firm of the Year" in 2002. LeBoeuf was ranked fifth in overall insurance M&A deals in 2002, advising on 24 transactions worth $9.7 billion, and first in M&A deals in 2002 in the property and casualty and life and health sectors with seven deals worth $1.5 billion.

The energy group has been one of the firm's strongest in the 21st century, participating in and completing 22 industry-related M&A deals for $67.7 billion since 1999. In May 2003, LeBoeuf was named "U.S. Energy Law Firm of the Year" by legal publishing group Chambers & Partners.

LeBoeuf also handles M&A advisory, public and private securities offerings, private equity and venture capital, among other engagements. The firm can boast of handling M&A transactions worth $500 billion in the last three years.

GETTING HIRED

Insiders report that LeBoeuf is tweaking its hiring process and "focusing more on a core group of elite schools." "[LeBoeuf] seems to be getting more and more competitive," according to one associate. "The range of law schools from which the firm recruits appears to be getting smaller." What schools are in favor? "They look at the big name East Coast schools and at the New York schools," says a source. There are few surprises in the actual process. "For law students, different attorneys from the office interview on campus and then call back certain students for further interviews with at least three other attorneys – usually half a day total," according to a source. "The usual criteria regarding schools, GPA, experience and the ability to conduct oneself are important," says a third-year. This source adds that "knowing a bit about the firm and what kind of clients it has is very helpful as well."

OUR SURVEY SAYS

LeBoeuf associates tell of a culture that is more informal at branch offices than the New York headquarters. "The culture in the branch offices is friendly and professional," says an attorney at a U.S. satellite office. "Lawyers tend to socialize together. There is good camaraderie among the various offices, with the exception of the main office." "The culture is a tad uptight," a Big Apple attorney concedes. "There is no overt tension between the attorneys, and they conduct themselves politely and professionally, but the atmosphere is extremely chilly."

Associates agree that LeBoeuf is competitive with regard to compensation. "The firm tries to meet the market in terms of compensation," says one attorney. "It is never a market leader and tries to stay comfortably within the pack." "The base salary is at or near the top, and the bonus is reasonable in light of the hour requirements," another associate happily reports. One compensation complaint is a hazy bonus structure. "Bonus criteria are a mystery," according to one contact. "The firm sets a billable hour requirement, but it is often not made known until after the year exactly what non-collectible matters will count as billable hours for bonus purposes."

Hours at LeBoeuf are reasonable, though some complain the firm is placing more demands on associates' schedules. Insiders also warn of varied and unpredictable hours. "The hours here are typical of other large firms, perhaps a little better," reports one source. "This used to be a quality of life firm. Now the firm has become fixated on billing. We're nicely compensated though." Another contact expounds on that: "Although LeBoeuf is sometimes dubbed a lifestyle firm, there is no question that those days are long gone. There is an increasing emphasis on the number of hours billed, and low billers are definitely getting the message."

The quality and availability of training at LeBoeuf varies by department. "There is no training for first-year litigators," says one associate in that department, a criticism the firm has addressed through the formation of a new litigation training program for its new arrivals. There's an informal mentoring program for junior associates called "LeBuddy." It's not universally loved. "The informal LeBuddy mentoring program is a joke," growls one contact. "My LeBuddy, while a nice person, has absolutely no professional interests or goals in common with me."

Linklaters

1345 Avenue of the Americas
19th Floor
New York, NY 10105
Phone: (212) 424-9000
www.linklaters.com

LOCATIONS

New York, NY* • Alicante •
Amsterdam • Antwerp • Bangkok*
• Beijing* • Berlin • Bratislava •
Brussels • Bucharest • Budapest •
Cologne • Frankfurt* • Hong
Kong* • Lisbon • London* •
Luxembourg • Madrid* • Milan •
Moscow* • Munich • Paris* •
Prague • Rome* • São Paulo* •
Shanghai • Singapore* •
Stockholm • Tokyo* • Warsaw

*Office with U.S. practice
capability*

THE STATS

No. of attorneys firm-wide:
2,000+
No. of attorneys in New York: 55+
No. of offices: 30
Summer associate offers firm wide:
16 out of 16 (2003)
**Summer associate offers in New
York:** 9 out of 9 (2003)
Senior Partner: Anthony Cann
Managing Partner: Tony Angel

UPPERS

• International prestige with growing U.S. practice
• Reasonable hours and market pay

DOWNERS

• Little name recognition in the U.S.
• Confusing bonus sytem

NOTABLE PERKS

• Attorney retreats held all around the world
• Free espresso, great chocolate chip cookies and Friday drink cart
• 12-week paid maternity leave
• Discounted gym membership

MAJOR DEPARTMENTS & PRACTICES

Asset Finance*
Banking*
Capital Markets*
Corporate*/M&A
Employment, Pensions & Incentives
Environment & Planning
EU/Competition
Financial Markets
Intellectual Property
Investment Management
IT & Communications
Litigation & Arbitration*
Projects*
Real Estate & Construction
Restructuring & Insolvency*
Tax*

* *Practice areas covered by U.S.*
practice

EMPLOYMENT CONTACT

Mr. Michael McEvoy
Recruitment Coordinator
Phone: (212) 632-9859
Fax: (212) 424-9100
E-mail:
uspractice.recruitment@linklaters.com

BASE SALARY

New York, NY
1st year: $125,000
2nd year: $135,000
3rd year: $150,000
4th year: $170,000
5th year: $190,000
6th year: $205,000
7th year: $220,000
8th year: $230,000
Summer associate: $2,404/week

THE SCOOP

It's here. It's there. It's everywhere. Prestigious international law firm Linklaters has over 2,000 lawyers in 30 offices across the globe. The firm's empire includes Western and Eastern Europe, Asia and its sole U.S. office in New York whose 50-plus lawyers handle asset finance, banking, capital markets, litigation, restructuring and insolvency, structured finance and tax.

Looking for glamorous international work? Linklaters has it. The firm's asset finance team just received two Deal of the Year awards from *Asset Finance International* for a series of five QTE financings worth $1.5 billion and for a U.S./Portuguese double-dip financing of $135 million for Metro do Porto. The firm also represented a major Brazilian bank in a note issued by its special purpose company in the Cayman Islands and worked on a $500 million debt restructuring for the City of Buenos Aires, following Argentina's economic crisis.

In July 2003, four litigators from Shearman & Sterling – Paul Wickes, James Warnot, Mary Warren and Amanda Gallagher – joined the Linklaters family as partners. A few months later, Linklaters welcomed former Latham & Watkins partner Martin Flics, who joined the restructuring and insolvency practice, and David Deck from Shearman, who joined the U.S. practice in Tokyo. But it hasn't been all growth and smiles. The firm lost Marianne Rosenberg, head of the U.S. general finance team, to Thelen Reid & Priest in 2003 in the wake of a June 2003 article in *The Lawyer* that reported unrest among partners over the issue of aggressive recruiting of lateral partners.

GETTING HIRED

Pedigree and international experience are key at Linklaters. "The firm shops the Ivy schools and is looking for students at the top of their class, but there is also an emphasis on cultural fit within the firm," says a source. "People with significant international experience – personal or professional – tend to be well represented here. I expect it will become more competitive as Linklaters builds a stronger U.S. presence." "Although Linklaters is not well known among people interested in purely domestic law," the firm is famous among internationally minded law students at top schools. "It is, after all, one of the – if not the – most prestigious firms in the world," points out one insider.

OUR SURVEY SAYS

Don't expect an office full of robots: insiders say Linklaters' New York office is a laid-back place filled with an eclectic mix of individuals. "Linklaters is a friendly office with interesting people," says one lawyer. "[It's] definitely not a place with cookie-cutter lawyers. Most people have quirky backgrounds and interests that make them great to talk to and fabulous to work with. People are creative about work and their lives in general." Some say the firm has a tea-and-crumpets feel. "The culture is very English," says one contact, who goes on to say "Most people are very friendly, though also a bit reserved. Almost everyone is upbeat and seems to enjoy their work." Some associates have pen pals all over the world. "I feel that I have close friends throughout the firm in cities across the globe, from London, Brussels and Warsaw to São Paulo, Singapore and Tokyo," says one international social butterfly.

Insiders report that compensation at Linklaters is "competitive with top-tier New York firms." "Compensation is on par with the usual suspects of top New York law firms," says one contact, and others point out that "while abroad, the firm offers a very generous cost of living allowance." Bonuses at Linklaters are merit-based, but some say the specifics of the bonus scheme are arcane. "I have not figured out how the bonus structure works, other than it is supposed to be competitive to our peers," says one baffled source.

Attorneys at Linklaters work hard, but the firm is by no means billables-obsessed. "When I need to work hard or late, I do," says a junior associate. "But the firm is very respectful of people's personal lives as well, and when I need to leave the office, I do that too. I don't feel pressure to bill." Reports one source, "My hours have never been an issue and there is never any pressure to put in any face time. As long as you get things done, nobody is knocking on your door asking you to bill more hours."

Linklaters gets high marks for its commitment to pro bono work. Says one associate, "The firm is very committed to pro bono and strongly encourages people to get actively involved in the community," while another Linklaters associate points out that each year an award is given at the firm's holiday party for pro bono work within the firm.

Mayer, Brown, Rowe & Maw

1675 Broadway
New York, NY 10019-5820
Phone: (212) 506-2500
Fax: (212) 262-1910
www.mayerbrownrowe.com

LOCATIONS

Chicago, IL (HQ)
Charlotte, NC
Houston, TX
Los Angeles, CA
New York, NY
Palo Alto, CA
Washington, DC
Beijing*
Brussels
Cologne
Frankfurt
London
Manchester
Paris
Shanghai*

* Representative offices

THE STATS

No. of attorneys firm-wide: 1,350
No. of attorneys in New York: 225
No. of offices: 13
Managing Partner: Debora de Hoyos
Hiring Partner: Kathleen A. Walsh

UPPERS

- Prestigious appellate practice
- Global reach, big-name clients

DOWNERS

- Intense billable hours target
- Senior associates can hog hours and quality cases

NOTABLE PERKS

- Free doughnuts
- Subsidized BlackBerrys
- Discount gym memberships
- Annual firm-wide outing

MAJOR DEPARTMENTS & PRACTICES

Bankruptcy & Reorganization
Corporate & Securities
Finance
Intellectual Property
Litigation
Real Estate
Tax Transactions

EMPLOYMENT CONTACT

Ms. Frances Vaughn
Associate Recruitment Manager
Phone: (212) 506-2799
Fax: (212) 262-1910
E-mail:
fvaughn@mayerbrownrowe.com

BASE SALARY

New York, NY
1st year: $125,000
2nd year: $135,000
3rd year: $150,000
4th year: $170,000
5th year: $190,000
6th year: $205,000
7th year: $215,000
8th year: $225,000
9th year: $235,000
Summer associate: $2,400/week

THE SCOOP

A transatlantic power, Mayer Brown Rowe & Maw is the product of the union between Chicago-based Mayer, Brown & Platt and London-based Rowe & Maw. The 2002 merger created an international firm with 1,350 lawyers in 13 offices. Despite initial skepticism about the coupling, a 2003 survey in *Legal Week* named the combo the most successful transatlantic merger, narrowly beating Clifford Chance Rogers & Wells.

The firm serves 65 of the Fortune 100 companies and one out of every three U.S. banks. Firm clients include such heavy-hitters as Abbott Laboratories, AIG, Bank of America, Bertelsmann, Deutsche Bank, Dow Chemical, Ernst & Young, GE, Morgan Stanley, Nestlé, Pfizer and United Airlines.

Mayer Brown has advised on such transactions as the $2.6 billion purchase of a new product line by Nestlé Holdings, Security Capital's $5.5 billion merger with GE Capital, and Donna Karan International's merger with LVMG Moet Hennessy-Louis Vuitton. The firm's litigators are representing 19 oil companies in a suit against the U.S. Department of Defense, seeking a combined $2.5 billion for underpayment in military jet fuel contracts and recently won a U.S. Supreme Court case on behalf of Chevron Oil affirming an employer's hiring discretion. The firm's appellate practice has argued more than 30 cases in front of the high court since 1995 – more than any other firm.

GETTING HIRED

"Our firm basically interviews at the best law schools," says one associate, though the firm points out that it also interviews at local schools. The requirements are typical. "Mayer Brown, like the other big firms, likes the top candidates, and I think a big emphasis is placed on one's statistics, and particularly one's school," says one source. "The economy may have even ratcheted up the standards more." Another contact spells out the standards. "High GPA, law review and/or other activities and, depending on the practice group, prior work experience are all helpful." Sources suggest that "expertise, intellectual sophistication and real experience are more important than the law school you attend. This is not a stepping stone firm – the firm wants candidates who want to work here and be part of the team."

OUR SURVEY SAYS

Mayer Brown associates say the firm is a "civil and polite" place to work. "The culture is professional, cordial and collegial, with only rare exceptions," says one source. "Courtesy and team work are emphasized. There are lots of opportunities for lawyers to socialize for those that want to, but it is not required." "The culture at Mayer Brown New York is relatively laid back," says a senior associate. "Partners are extremely accessible, and their doors are almost always open." Some insiders feel there is a layer of formality, but it comes with the territory. "The culture here is on the whole pretty friendly, but, of course, a certain degree of uptightness is built into any firm," reports one lawyer. "I mean, my god, we're talking about lawyers here. We certainly don't sit around shooting the shit with partners or anything, but would you want to?"

Mayer Brown has improved its compensation structure, much to the pleasure of its associates. "This year, our bonus was at the higher end of comparable firms in the New York market," says one insider. "In prior years, the bonus was significantly lower than comparable firms." "While not historically the case, the firm currently seeks to match, and on occasion exceeds, the market," reports another lawyer. (The firm points out that in the 2002 bonus cycle, the New York office adopted a lock-step bonus policy.) That doesn't mean there aren't a few complainers. "Bonuses are lame – entirely based on hours, except for a discretionary bonus for extraordinary circumstances," says one contact. "Basic message to associates is that no one cares about quality of work."

Mayer Brown is one of the few firms with a "free-market" work assignment system, where associates seek out cases rather than having work handed to them. The system has its advantages and disadvantages. Reports one insider, "You can choose which partners and areas of specialty you are interested in working with. However, it is a 'swim or sink' approach, especially for junior associates because if fewer partners choose you to be their right hand, you will not meet the minimum 2,100-hour requirement." Watch out for case-hogs. "Because this is a free-market system and bonuses are driven by hours, there can be work distribution problems," complains a junior associate. "Senior and midlevel [associates] have [a] tendency to hog work in order to get maximum bonuses, often at the expense of juniors getting a sufficient workload."

Milbank, Tweed, Hadley & McCloy LLP

One Chase Manhattan Plaza
New York, NY 10005
Phone: (212) 530-5000
www.milbank.com

LOCATIONS

New York, NY (HQ)
Los Angeles, CA
Palo Alto, CA
Washington, DC
Frankfurt
Hong Kong
London
Singapore
Tokyo

THE STATS

No. of attorneys firm-wide: 516
No. of attorneys in New York: 329
No. of offices: 9
Summer associate offers firm-wide:
49 out of 52 (2003)
Summer associate offers in New York: 35 out of 37 (2003)
Chairman: Mel Immergut
Hiring Partners: Drew Fine, Jay Grushkin, Dan Bartfeld

UPPERS

- Sophisticated, high-level work
- Have you seen those views?!

DOWNERS

- Sink-or-swim attitude about training
- Penny-pinching

NOTABLE PERKS

- Part-time option for parents
- Same-sex partner benefits
- In-firm subsidized cafeteria
- Four-weeks paternity leave
- Technology bonus

MAJOR DEPARTMENTS & PRACTICES

Banking
Capital Markets
Communications & Space
Corporate
Financial Restructuring
High Yield & Acquisition Finance
Intellectual Property
Litigation
Mergers & Acquisitions
Power & Energy
Project Finance
Real Estate
Securitization
Tax
Technology
Transportation Finance
Trusts & Estates

EMPLOYMENT CONTACT

Ms. June Chotoo
Recruiting Coordinator
Phone: (212) 530-8322
Fax: (212) 822-8322
E-mail: jchotoo@milbank.com

BASE SALARY

New York, NY
1st year: $125,000
2nd year: $135,000
3rd year: $150,000
4th year: $165,000
5th year: $190,000
6th year: $205,000
7th year: $215,000
8th year: $225,000
Summer associate: $2,403/week

THE SCOOP

Founded in 1866, Milbank, Tweed, Hadley & McCloy is a big player on Wall Street that has long had an international bend as well. The firm has had significant operations in Asia since 1925, that are involved in high-provile and complex cross-border financings. Milbank is also extremely active throughout Latin America, where it has been recognized as the No. 1 legal advisor in the region by several industry periodicals. The project finance practice at Milbank, which focuses on infrastructure and energy projects in developing nations, is routinely recognized as an industry leader as well.

The firm's financial restructuring group has been engaged in many high-profile bankruptcies, including legal work on the Enron case, which has proved a financial boon for Milbank and other firms. Milbank submitted a bill for $24.2 million worth of legal services in November 2002. Creditors are fretting that high legal bills will significantly reduce the value of Enron assets available, and a court-appointed committee has called for fees claimed by Milbank to be reduced by 5.2 percent.

Does the name William Webster sound familiar? Webster, a long-time Milbank partner who has held positions as a federal appeals court judge, FBI director and head of the CIA, was named to another high-profile post when the Securities and Exchange Commission chose him to head an oversight board charged with keeping Enron-like corporate scandals at bay. Webster is part of a litigation department that has grown five-fold in the last seven years.

GETTING HIRED

Pedigree is an important factor in landing a spot at Milbank. Insiders say that the firm places an increasing emphasis on hiring associates from the top law schools. "There is a heavy emphasis on where the candidate went to law school and grades," says a litigator. "The partnership has apparently decided to make getting a job here far, far harder than it's been in years past." One associate claims Milbank seeks "nicey-nicey, solid, steady types. There is a lot of emphasis on social niceties." Says another associate, "I've seen [Milbank] turn down people who looked very good on paper, but were lifeless in person. I think the attitude is that there are a lot of people who are capable of doing this work, but they want to find people they can stand to work with, too." Warns another attorney, "Being able to fit in is important."

OUR SURVEY SAYS

Insiders state that the internal culture at Milbank "heavily depends on the group with whom one is associated." Some practices come in for praise; the intellectual property group, for example, is said to "rock." IP is "an extremely satisfying place to be, mostly because of the relationship between the people in the group," explains one insider. Corporate and leasing are also said to be particularly social. However, the firm is said to be "friendly but distant" overall.

Milbank's New York office is known for its breathtaking views. "The views of the Statue of Liberty and Manhattan Island, looking north, are spectacular," marvels one associate in that office. New York associates have plenty of time to relish those magnificent vistas, since "all offices are exterior." As an added bonus, "Associates only share offices for their first year." Milbank associates enjoy all the largesse of a major law firm. One insider cites some attractive perks. "We get typical large-firm stuff – bar expenses and association fees are paid; cars home at night; transit program and medical pre-tax spending program; 401(k); in-firm subsidized cafeteria; subsidized health club program; group lunches once a week; Super Bowl parties, golf outings and much more." Associates also "get four weeks of paternity leave" and "$2,000 in the first year as a technological bonus."

Some associates have been working fewer hours lately – but they're not necessarily happy about that fact. One corporate associate expresses dissatisfaction "because, like many corporate associates, I billed very few hours [in 2002]. That led to a lower bonus. In fact, I understand that only one associate in the corporate finance group (consisting of about 80 attorneys) billed over 2,000 hours last year. We can't learn if we don't have deals on which to work." A project finance pro has had a somewhat different experience. "You have to work really hard when deals are hot or are closing. On the other hand, I have very little pressure to do any face time, and billing hours are not mentioned too many times except at bonus time."

Milbank has historically been one of the most welcoming firms toward gays and lesbians. That laudable legacy continues. Says one insider, "Milbank is very upfront about being proud of its history in extending health and insurance benefits to same-sex domestic partners. It is extremely welcoming of gay associates and partners."

Milberg Weiss Bershad Hynes & Lerach LLP

One Pennsylvania Plaza
New York, NY 10119-0165
Phone: (212) 594-5300
www.milberg.com

LOCATIONS

New York, NY (HQ)
Boca Raton, FL
Los Angeles, CA
Philadelphia, PA
San Diego, CA
San Francisco, CA
Seattle, WA
Washington, DC

THE STATS

No. of attorneys firm-wide: 200+
No. of attorneys in New York: 81
No. of offices: 8
Summer associate offers in New York: 4 out of 4 (2003)

UPPERS

- High-profile plaintiffs' work and prestigious cases
- Associates like being on the 'good' side

DOWNERS

- Sink-or-swim attitude toward training
- Bonuses lag behind defense firms

NOTABLE PERKS

- Order food at firm's expense on Seamless Web
- Car service

MAJOR DEPARTMENTS & PRACTICES

Antitrust
Consumer Litigation
Insurance
Securities

EMPLOYMENT CONTACT

For summer associates:
Ms. Elaine Kusel or Mr. Dan Scotti
Recruiting Managers
Phone: (212) 415-8590
E-mail: hr@milberg.com

BASE SALARY

New York, NY
1st year: $125,000
Summer associate: $2,250/week (2L),
$1,700/week (1L)

THE SCOOP

Milberg Weiss Bershad Hynes & Lerach LLP is the largest plaintiff's contingency fee-based law firm in the nation, with more than 200 attorneys in eight offices – not to mention a support staff that includes forensic accountants, investigators and damage analysts. Founded in 1965, the firm has been responsible for more than $30 billion in aggregate recoveries. It represented plaintiffs in the first accounting fraud class action under federal securities laws more than 30 years ago and has consistently been a leader in prosecuting securities fraud ever since. Milberg Weiss lawyers put together $2 billion in settlements for investors defrauded by Drexel Burnham and Michael Milken and, in the American Continental/Lincoln Savings case, won a $1 billion jury award against those defendants who had not taken part in the $250 million settlement the firm had previously negotiated.

In February 2002, Milberg Weiss became lead counsel in the securities fraud suits against fallen energy giant Enron. Two months later, the firm filed a consolidated class-action lawsuit in Houston federal district court, charging certain executives and directors with engaging in massive insider trading (20 million shares with a sales price of roughly $1.2 billion) while making false and misleading public statements about the company's financial performance. Led by William Lerach, the Milberg Weiss team interviewed more than 100 witnesses and uncovered extensive evidence of document destruction by Enron auditor Andersen. The case is pending.

GETTING HIRED

"In light of the number of corporate scandals in recent times," says a third-year associate, "Milberg Weiss has been able to benefit from the publicity and hire some great people who also received offers from the biggest and best defense firms." Although the firm "has historically hired only laterals," according to insiders, it recently has launched a new summer associate program. But our sources say it's tough to get in, as the roster "seems to be all Harvard, Columbia, Georgetown and so on." Among the associates, "there are some from less prestigious local New York law schools and some from top schools who really want to do high-level plaintiffs' work." Because of the "heavy securities litigation practice," a midlevel associate advises, "A securities or financial background – even if just in law school classes – is a plus but not dispositive."

OUR SURVEY SAYS

"I love the work I do," enthuses a junior associate. "It is rewarding, I feel like I'm on the 'good' side and I am learning unbelievable amounts with the hands-on experience." Another warns, "You are expected to be able to jump right in and draft a complaint, write a brief and so on with little guidance. In that respect, you are forced to learn really quickly. It's pretty much sink-or-swim." She adds, "If you'd rather write memos and do document review for your first couple years before you are responsible for a whole complaint or brief yourself, then go to a large corporate-side firm where you will get more training."

Insiders describe the vibe at the firm as "relatively laid-back." But they also point out that "there is a certain degree of tension in the air at all times." Some report that "the plaintiffs' side seems to attract more laid-back, interesting – i.e. quirky – people who often are socially conscious rather than just in it for the money. People are not pretentious or into being high-powered New York lawyers." Sources also appreciate that "casual dress is the norm, and it is more casual than business casual at other firms."

"The hours can suck," admits one attorney frankly. Cases are usually staffed with one partner and one associate, so "often you are the only associate doing all the work on a case, unless it's one of the big, high-profile ones." Fortunately, "the majority of the partners are very laid-back and really treat the associates like colleagues rather than underlings." Still, "the partners are not always good about understanding that you have work to do for somebody else and you often get stuck in the middle of a dispute on whose work you do first."

The compensation at Milberg Weiss "is comparable to defense firms," one source reports, "but some associates are able to negotiate more money." Another insider agrees that "everybody is not paid the same" and feels "this can cause some strife in the associate ranks." She also says that while "the pay is close to that of the big New York corporate firms," Milberg Weiss is "not close on the bonuses."

Morgan & Finnegan

345 Park Avenue
New York, NY 10154-0053
Phone: (212) 758-4800
www.morganfinnegan.com

LOCATIONS

New York, NY (HQ)
Washington, DC

THE STATS

No. of attorneys firm-wide: 103
No. of attorneys in New York: 95
No. of offices: 2
Summer associate offers in New York*: 12 out of 14 (2003)
(Summer program in NY only)
Managing Partner: Executive Committee
Hiring Partner: Tony V. Pezzano

MAJOR DEPARTMENTS & PRACTICES

Biotechnology
Chemicals/Pharmaceuticals
Computers/Electronics/
  Telecommunications
E-commerce & Financial Systems
Mechanical/Medical
Nanotechnology
Trademark, Copyright, Unfair
  Competition & Trade Secrets

EMPLOYMENT CONTACT

Ms. Suzanne Krebs
Manager of Legal Recruiting
E-mail: skrebs@morganfinnegan.com

THE SCOOP

The IP landscape has changed in the last century, but New York-based Morgan & Finnegan has changed with it. Founded in 1893, the firm's intellectual property practice includes litigation and prosecution matters involving such areas as biotechnology, chemicals/pharmaceuticals, computers/electronics/telecommunications, e-commerce and financial systems, medical/mechanical devices, nanotechnology, trademarks, copyrights, unfair competition and trade secrets. Ninety percent of the firm's more than 100 attorneys practice in New York.

Morgan & Finnegan services a broad spectrum of clients from Fortune 500 companies to emerging companies and individual entrepreneurs. Among the companies the firm has represented are Bombardier, ChevronTexaco, DuPont, Fujitsu, Hoffmann-La Roche, IBM, Procter & Gamble, Rolex, Toyota Industries and W.L. Gore & Associates, as well as government agencies such as the National Institutes of Health.

Morgan & Finnegan does a great deal of pro bono work. The firm is representing a former New York City bus driver who was forced to leave her job by the Metropolitan Transit Authority because she suffers from multiple sclerosis. The firm has worked on employment and housing discrimination, criminal appeals and political asylum cases and has represented groups like the Rainforest Alliance, the Center for Employment Opportunities and the Vera Institute of Justice.

GETTING HIRED

M&F has a simple formula for hiring associates. "A great school, transcript and writing sample will win the day," says an insider, who adds that the "interview is mostly a check to see if you fit in with firm culture." The firm's IP focus comes into play. "Morgan & Finnegan wants associates who are interested in technology, who are serious about work and who have outside interests as well," says one attorney. Some associates warn that different interviewers will have different criteria. "The firm does not have a consistent approach regarding what credentials are important," says that source. "Some attorneys place a huge emphasis on the applicant's law school, while others focus on if the applicant is a team player and would fit in at the firm."

OUR SURVEY SAYS

Most Morgan & Finnegan insiders agree that "the firm is laid-back, informal and very friendly. Morgan & Finnegan treats you as a professional and expects the same in return." Things can get serious when the need arises. "We tailor our culture depending on the setting," says a source. "We act appropriately in court and in front of clients. Depending on the nature of the meeting, we notch up or down the formality. But in general, we get to be fairly casual." "Morgan & Finnegan is a Park Avenue firm without the white-shoe philosophy," says one contact. "Dress code is casual dress full time. Associates are very friendly and always willing to assist if needed." Those who fear an "Et tu, Brute?" moment will be relieved to hear the firm has "very few back stabbers." However, some complain that junior associates are in the dark about important firm issues and bemoan "the level of secrecy the partnership maintains regarding the business issues of the firm."

The firm's hours requirement isn't unreasonable, and pressure to bill is far from significant. "There is a minimum billable requirement of 2,000 hours, but that is not difficult to hit," reports one associate. "The pressure to bill is there, as it is at all firms, but no one has harassed me – at least, not so far – about increasing my billables," reports another contact. Insiders say the 2,000 mark "is rarely mentioned" except in yearly reviews. "People know and do what is expected," shrugs one lawyer.

Complaints about M&F's somewhat unusual compensation structure are frequent. "The compensation is great, compared to other professions," says one lawyer. "Relative to other law firms of this caliber, [it's] only okay." Salaries are lock-step for junior associates. But at "higher levels, compensation depends mostly on your negotiation skills." That doesn't sit too well with associates. "Morgan & Finnegan's reluctance to pay lock-step salaries and bonuses keeps it from joining the ranks of elite law firms," gripes one source. "To put it nicely, Morgan & Finnegan's compensation decisions are reactionary and not well thought out."

"The training here is excellent," says one attorney. "During the summers, there are several classes on IP, which are extremely helpful if you've never taken an IP class in law school." It's not just summer associates who take advantage of the excellent training. "The Morgan & Finnegan in-house CLE program provides a strong foundation for both patent litigation and prosecution."

Morgan, Lewis & Bockius LLP

101 Park Avenue
New York, NY 10178-0060
Phone: (212) 309-6000
www.morganlewis.com

LOCATIONS

Boston, MA • Chicago, IL •
Harrisburg, PA • Irvine, CA • Los
Angeles, CA • Miami, FL • New
York, NY • Northern Virginia • Palo
Alto, CA • Philadelphia, PA •
Pittsburgh, PA • Princeton, NJ •
San Francisco, CA • Washington,
DC • Brussels • Frankfurt • London
• Tokyo

THE STATS

No. of attorneys firm-wide: 1,178
No. of attorneys in New York: 285
No. of offices: 18
Summer associate offers firm-wide:
62 out of 72 (2003)
**Summer associate offers in New
York:** 17 out of 21 (2003)
Firm Chair: Francis M. Milone
Hiring Partners: Eric Kraeutler
(Firm-wide); Christopher T. Jensen,
Michele A. Coffey (NY)

UPPERS

- Unsurpassed presence in New York,
  Philadelphia and DC
- Reasonable hours requirements

DOWNERS

- Long hours
- Not a pace setter for associate
  salaries

NOTABLE PERKS

- Bar expenses
- Firm-sponsored socials, such as
  black-tie dinner dance
- Monthly cocktail parties
- Practice group ski trips

MAJOR DEPARTMENTS & PRACTICES

Antitrust
Bankruptcy
Business & Finance
Employee Benefits & Executive
  Compensation
Environmental
Finance & Financial Restructuring
Intellectual Property
Labor & Employment Law
Litigation
Mergers & Acquisitions
Patent Litigation
Real Estate
Securities
Tax
Technology
TECI (Torts, Environmental,
  Construction & Insurance)

EMPLOYMENT CONTACT

Ms. Susan Reonegro
Recruiting Manager
Phone: (212) 309-6000
Fax: (212) 309-6001

BASE SALARY

New York, NY
Class of 2002: $125,000
Class of 2001: $135,000
Class of 2000: $150,000
Class of 1999: $167,000
Class of 1998: $187,000
Class of 1997: $200,000
Summer associate: $27,000/summer

THE SCOOP

If size matters, then Morgan, Lewis & Bockius LLP matters a lot. The firm ranks among the 10 largest U.S. law firms with nearly 1,200 lawyers in 18 offices worldwide. The firm has approximately 300 lawyers each in legal hot spots New York, Washington, D.C., and Philadelphia, and is the only law firm to have such extensive coverage in all three cities. The firm has also expanded on the West Coast, since signing on 60 partners from the former Brobeck, Phleger & Harrison.

Morgan Lewis has grown strategically over the past few years. The firm boosted its patent practice with the addition of 35 lawyers from Hopgood Calimafde Judlowe & Mondolino, an IP boutique firm, in 2001. In 2003, the firm signed on 150 lawyers from the former Brobeck, Phleger & Harrison. Also in 2003, Morgan Lewis expanded its insurance recovery practice with the addition of 27 lawyers from Zevnik Horton, a move that prompted the opening of the firm's new Chicago and Boston offices.

In 2001, Morgan Lewis launched the Public Interest and Community Service program, which allows summer associates to participate in the traditional full summer experience at the firm or to spend part of their summer on a full-time assignment with a non-profit organization, while receiving full compensation from the firm.

GETTING HIRED

Thanks in part to the rough economy, Morgan Lewis can afford to be more selective than ever before. The firm hires "people with strong academic backgrounds who communicate well and are looking for the opportunity to take on responsibility." "We are definitely a 'fit' firm. Someone may have great credentials, but may not fit with our culture, and they may not get an offer where someone with a less 'superstar' resume may get an offer if they seem like they will be a good team player." A senior associate has observed that "summer associate hiring is becoming more competitive than perhaps in the past, to make it more likely that the summer associate experience will be more productive and more likely to lead to full-time offers." "I think it is particularly difficult now with the slow economy. MLB interviews at the top law schools and tends to be pretty exclusive," a fourth-year reveals.

OUR SURVEY SAYS

"The quality of life for an associate at Morgan Lewis is good," says one source. "I would say that the firm culture is friendly." "I find the work challenging and intellectually stimulating," enthuses one insider. "The attorneys I work with are bright, efficient, motivated and take a genuine interest in my professional development." On rare occasions, partners have been known to raise their voices. "I have seen a small number of senior partners berate and yell at associates and law clerks," says a contact. (The firm points out that it has a no tolerance policy for screamers.) "The partners poorly communicate issues, comments and information to associates," complains one attorney. Still, one associate points out, "Problems with partners exist at every firm, but I think these sorts of problems are few and fairly far between at Morgan Lewis."

Like their counterparts at top firms across the nation, Morgan Lewis associates work long hours. "There is no doubt that I work a lot of hours as an associate here and that I would work much less in most other professions," explains one associate. "Some weeks or months are especially grueling and my personal life suffers. But I choose to practice law in a large firm, and with the benefits come the hours," remarks another insider. "The hours are not unreasonable – far from it, in fact – and most attorneys appreciate and respect the fact that people have lives outside of the office," agrees another contact.

Most Morgan Lewis associates feel the firm is fair when it comes to compensation. "I feel my compensation is generally consistent with the best firms in the city," says one New York associate. "I don't think the firm strives to be the pacesetter in New York for associate salaries, but I don't think that is a negative, as I think that the firm is more than competitive salary-wise." Although most New Yorkers appear satisfied with their base salary, the prevailing opinion seems to be that the firm "is not as generous with bonuses as other firms."

Morgan Lewis associates appreciate their firm's commitment to attorney development and training. The "helpful" formal training programs are available "at least two times a month." "But the real value," opines one New Yorker, "is in the real-world experience you can obtain at this firm." Moreover, there is "ample opportunity to participate in outside CLE courses."

O'Melveny & Myers LLP

Citigroup Center
153 East 53rd Street
54th Floor
New York, NY 10022-4611
Phone: (212) 326-2000

30 Rockefeller Plaza
New York, NY 10112
Phone: (212) 408-2400
www.omm.com

LOCATIONS

Century City, CA • Irvine, CA • Los
Angeles, CA • New York, NY •
Newport Beach, CA • San
Francisco, CA • Silicon Valley, CA
• Washington, DC • Beijing • Hong
Kong • London • Shanghai • Tokyo

THE STATS

No. of attorneys firm-wide: 900 +
No. of attorneys in New York: 216
No. of offices: 13
Summer associate offers firm-wide:
127 out of 139 (2003)
**Summer associate offers in New
York:** 22 out of 23 (2003)
Chairman: Arthur B. Culvahouse Jr.
Hiring attorney: Carla
Christofferson

UPPERS

- Collegial co-workers
- Challenging, sophisticated work

DOWNERS

- Increasing emphasis on billable hours
- Little in the way of formal training

NOTABLE PERKS

- Free wireless e-mail
- Family circus event
- Overtime meals

MAJOR DEPARTMENTS & PRACTICES

Intellectual Property & Technology
Labor & Employment
Litigation
Tax
Transactions

EMPLOYMENT CONTACT

Ms. Jill Mersel
New York Director of Legal Personnel
Phone: (212) 408-2457
Fax: (212) 408-2420
E-mail: jmersel@omm.com

BASE SALARY

New York, NY
1st year: $125,000
2nd year: $135,000
3rd year: $150,000
4th year: $170,000
5th year: $190,000
6th year: $205,000
7th year: $220,000
8th year: $230,000
Summer associate: $2,400/week

THE SCOOP

Things have never been better at O'Melveny & Myers. Founded in 1885 in Los Angeles, the firm is raking in record profits per partner and enjoying a period of great growth. OMM is known for its litigation work and also has prominent IP, labor and transaction practices.

In 2002, OMM merged with O'Sullivan LLP, a leader in private equity. The merger is already paying off; according to *Private Equity Analyst*, OMM ranked as the No. 1 law firm in private equity deals completed in the first half of 2003. The addition of O'Sullivan's 88 attorneys helped make OMM the 15th largest firm in the country, according to a survey by *The National Law Journal*. The firm now has two New York offices but will combine at a new space in the Times Square Tower in 2004.

OMM's litigators represent Unocal in a suit filed on behalf of a handful of Myanmar (Burma) villagers and an activist opposed to the ruling government. The suit alleges that Unocal is vicariously liable for conscripted labor and other human rights abuses allegedly committed by the Myanmar army during construction of a gas pipeline in which a Unocal affiliate invested. If plaintiffs are successful, the ramifications for American corporations conducting business in foreign jurisdictions could be enormous, with American corporations facing potential liability for acts of foreign governments against their own citizens for injuries incurred outside the U.S.

GETTING HIRED

Sources tell us that OMM is "fairly strict about hiring only from top-10 law schools and only the top of the class." "Lots of people with great grades still get dinged because of personality. We're very picky here and we're conscious of that," confides a litigator. Veteran insiders say the firm's criteria are only getting tougher. "Several current associates, including myself, have remarked that we don't think we would have been hired under the firm's current criteria," says a second-year associate. Other insiders tell us, "An outgoing personality never hurts." Indeed, "grades and academic qualifications are just the beginning. There has to be a social fit or you're out." But "the callback process is very laid-back with the interviewers really wanting to get to know the person – what it would be like to have that person as a colleague," reports a fourth-year.

OUR SURVEY SAYS

Many insiders at O'Melveny say it's impossible to identify a firm-wide culture. "I don't think there is a firm-wide culture. Rather, there are sub-department cultures," says an associate. "As a result of the O'Sullivan merger, there really is not one culture. The O'Sullivan culture was laid back and friendly, but the O'Melveny culture tends to be more bureaucratic and rigid," says a corporate associate.

Compensation at O'Melveny is "competitive with other major international law firms," associates report. "If you put in the hours, you will be rewarded," remarks one corporate associate." However, several insiders have a bone to pick with O'Melveny regarding bonuses. "The constantly changing bonus structure is bewildering, opaque and typically fails to meet the expectations that management created," a sixth-year insider states. Associates from several practice groups report a "tremendous pressure to meet billable-hour requirements" as of late, although the firm tells us that it has recently phased out such hours requirements.

"Partners are generous, supportive, helpful, self-deprecating and genuinely nice," shares a New York associate, who adds, "The ones I have worked with have been willing to stay as late as we have and have never dumped their work on us so they could go home early." However, some associates who say the partners are "open, friendly and available to answer questions" wish the partners were more proactive regarding mentoring and communication. A second-year opines, "Associates are treated with great respect when it comes to their work on legal matters. Associates' opinions regarding administrative and governance matters seem to be given less weight."

"The firm has a reasonably strong commitment to pro bono work," reveals a fourth-year. "All approved pro bono work – and approval does not appear to be a problem – counts toward annual minimum billable hours. There is no limit on the number of pro bono hours that will count toward billable hours." However, according to this source, "There is pressure to take on client billable hours that can interfere with the ability to actually get involved in the pro bono program."

Orrick, Herrington & Sutcliffe

666 Fifth Avenue
New York, NY 10103-0001
Phone: (212) 506-5000
www.orrick.com

LOCATIONS

Los Angeles, CA
New York, NY
Orange County, CA
Pacific Northwest (Seattle & Portland)
Sacramento, CA
San Francisco, CA
Silicon Valley (Menlo Park, CA)
Washington, DC
London
Milan
Paris
Tokyo

THE STATS

No. of attorneys firm-wide: 675+
No. of attorneys in New York:
190+
No. of offices: 12
Summer associate offers firm-wide:
52 out of 57 (2003)
**Summer associate offers in New
York:** 15 out of 17 (2003)
**Chairman and Chief Executive
Officer:** Ralph H. Baxter Jr.
Hiring Partners: Douglas Madsen
(Firm-wide), Lauren J. Elliot (New
York)

UPPERS

- Public finance superstars
- Culture of camaraderie

DOWNERS

- Bonuses tied to hours
- High hours expectations

NOTABLE PERKS

- Summer associate health club memberships
- Profit-sharing program
- Concierge service
- Monthly office cocktail parties

MAJOR DEPARTMENTS & PRACTICES

Bankruptcy & Debt Restructuring

Compensation & Benefits

Corporate

Employment Law

Energy & Project Finance

Institutional Finance, Banking &
 Private Investment Funds

Intellectual Property

Leasing

Litigation

Mergers & Acquisitions

Public Finance

Real Estate

Structured Finance

Tax

EMPLOYMENT CONTACT

Ms. Jennifer Youngquist

Law Students Contact

Phone: (212) 506-3553

Fax: (212) 506-5151

E-mail: jyoungquist@orrick.com

Ms. Francesca Runge

Lateral Contact

Phone: (212) 506-3556

Fax: (212) 506-5151

E-mail: frunge@orrick.com

BASE SALARY

New York, NY

1st year: $125,000

Summer associate: $10,400/month

THE SCOOP

Orrick, Herrington & Sutcliffe traces its roots back to 1863 San Francisco. The firm expanded in the 1980s and 1990s, opening a New York office in 1984. Today, the New York office is the firm's largest, with nearly 200 lawyers. The firm has continued its overseas growth in recent years, acquiring Paris and Milan offices in November 2002 and May 2003, respectively, and now has more than 675 lawyers in 12 offices around the world.

A leader in finance, the firm was honored as Top Bond Counsel and Top Underwriters by *The Bond Buyer* in 2001 and 2002 and was recently named U.S. Capital Markets Law Firm of the Year by Chambers & Partners.

Particularly well known for expertise in commercial litigation, employment law, product liability and intellectual property, the firm's litigators handle cases from state and federal trial courts to the U.S. Supreme Court. *The American Lawyer* named Orrick the second-ranked defense firm in the United States for IP cases in 2002, according to the number of times they were hired by defendants involved in patent cases filed in that year. The firm's corporate practice represents new and emerging companies as well as established technology-oriented corporations.

GETTING HIRED

"The process to get hired is more difficult these days," an Orrick source reports, echoing the thoughts of associates at top firms across the country. The firm has high pedigree and GPA standards (Orrick recruits at top-25 law firm feeders as well as good regional schools), but, says one associate, "Above all else, Orrick wants a candidate who is a strong cultural fit with the firm. Good grades and demonstrated work ethic are not enough. Orrick asks from the outset: 'Is this person partner material?'" The New York office may be at a slight disadvantage. "Orrick's recruitment is competitive, but at least in New York, still falls slightly behind other top firms due to the fact that it has only been in New York for 15 years instead of 50," suggests one contact. (Actually, the firm has been in the Big Apple for 20 years, but who's counting?)

OUR SURVEY SAYS

Orrick's laid-back, West Coast vibe permeates the entire firm, even in the heart of the Big Apple. The firm has a "laid-back attitude and is generally very respectful and flexible toward associates and staff, in part because of the firm's West Coast origins and the firm's formal 'core values' that are sincerely held by the firm's management," says one insider. "Orrick's the one place where congeniality and cooperation aren't just catchwords for recruitment brochures," brags one attorney. "Rather, they are genuine values attorneys see embraced and reinforced by colleagues every day. It's a wonderfully friendly, supportive, yet focused work environment, and the firm goes to great lengths to maintain that environment."

Orrick's monthly cocktail parties in New York are a hit, and associates appreciate the chance to relax with their colleagues in a social setting. "The shrimp at our cocktail parties are gigantic!" says one seafood-loving lawyer. "I think they might be grown hydroponically."

"Orrick strives to be competitive with regards to its compensation," says one associate. "Currently, associates are paid the same salary regardless of the office in which they work. Bonuses are determined based on 'PDC credit' hours, capped at 2,300 hours." (PDC credit hours include hours spent on client development and various professional development activities. In addition, all of an attorney's pro bono time counts toward their billable requirement and bonus eligibility.) For some particularly industrious types, the 2,300-hour ceiling is just too low. "The bonus structure provides compensation to 2,300 hours, but it is not uncommon for associates to be asked to bill over 2,500 hours," explains one hardworker.

"Orrick does focus on billable hours more than other firms, in that associates' bonuses are tightly tied to the number of hours billed," concedes one contact, "But I find that equitable, in that those who work harder are paid more." Another associate admits, "If you are going to be a lawyer in New York, there are a lot of worse places. However, I am not sure whether that is a function of the economy or the firm."

Orrick associates in New York appreciate that "recently the firm has begun a concerted effort to increase the frequency and range of formal training programs." Still, those insiders in the transactional practices tell us that "the bulk of the training takes place one-on-one in the context of actual transactions." Says one second-year associate, "I think the best training is performing the work."

Patterson, Belknap, Webb & Tyler LLP

1133 Avenue of the Americas
New York, NY 10036-6710
Phone: (212) 336-2000
www.pbwt.com

LOCATION

New York, NY

THE STATS

No. of attorneys: 176
No. of offices: 1
Summer associate offers: 11 out of 11 (2003)
Managing Partner: Rochelle Korman
Hiring Partner: Robert W. Lehrburger

UPPERS

- Reasonable hours
- Associates feel like "family"

DOWNERS

- Pay lags after year one
- Lack of formal training opportunities

NOTABLE PERKS

- $600 technology allowance
- Monthly scotch parties with pistachios and smoked salmon
- Four weeks paid paternal leave

MAJOR DEPARTMENTS & PRACTICES

Antitrust

Arbitration & Alternative Dispute
Resolution

Commonwealth of Independent
States

Complex Commercial Litigation

Corporate

Debtor-Creditor

Employment Law

Employee Benefits & Executive
Compensation

Intellectual Property

International Securities

Internet

Media & Entertainment

Products Liability

Real Estate

Securities & Commodities Litigation

Tax

Tax-Exempt Organizations

Trusts & Estates

White-Collar Criminal Defense &
Internal Investigations

EMPLOYMENT CONTACT

Ms. Robin L. Klum
Director of Professional Development
E-mail: rlklum@pbwt.com

BASE SALARY

New York, NY
1st year: $125,000
2nd year: $135,000
3rd year: $145,000
4th year: $155,000
5th year: $165,000
6th year: $175,000
Summer associate: $2,400/week

THE SCOOP

Patterson, Belknap, Webb & Tyler LLP is proof that it doesn't take a plethora of offices to have international reach. Founded in 1919, Patterson Belknap has 176 lawyers in its lone office in New York but its clients are located across the globe. The firm excels in the areas of commercial and corporate law and litigation.

In one of the firm's most important litigation cases, Patterson Belknap is representing Cendant, a travel and real estate service provider, in the company's lawsuit against Ernst & Young. Cendant was created through the merger of CUC International and HFS. After the merger, it was revealed that CUC International's management had manipulated financial statements to improve the appearance of the company's book. Cendant paid $3 billion to settle class-action suits filed by shareholders, then sued Ernst & Young, CUC International's accountant when the fraud was committed, charging the firm with fraud, negligence and breach of contract. The suit is pending.

Patterson Belknap is also well known for its pro bono service, logging over 24,000 pro bono hours in 2002. The firm has repeatedly been named the top New York law firm for pro bono work by *The American Lawyer*. Patterson Belknap attorneys have represented gratis criminal defendants, including death row inmates, on behalf of legal service providers, refugees seeking asylum in the United States and has assisted in investigations into persecution suffered by lawyers in Indonesia.

GETTING HIRED

Go-getters are valued. "Enthusiasm is a top factor, along with the ability to think creatively," says an associate. "We want applicants that are looking for a place to stand out rather than blend in; who want to be a name rather than a number. At the same time, our applicants have to know and appreciate the value of teamwork."

Some insiders worry that Patterson Belknap virtually ignores personality when making recruiting decisions. "Patterson Belknap is very willing to sacrifice personality for pedigree," complains one source. "At times, it becomes difficult to work with some people who have a wonderful educational pedigree but just zero personality. Some of the summers they have hired are painful to interact with!"

OUR SURVEY SAYS

Warm and fuzzy feelings abound at Patterson Belknap. "I have met some of my best friends at this firm. And even though it's unbearably cheesy, I think of my co-workers as a sort of family," says one midlevel associate. Family members say you won't have to worry about getting yelled at by mom or dad. "[The] atmosphere is very polite, [and] shouting is virtually nonexistent," reports a contact. "You worry more that people will be disappointed in you than that you'll get called on the carpet." But don't expect a party firm; the Patterson vibe is more relaxed than anything else. "The atmosphere is very cool, calm and relaxed," says one lawyer. "People are friendly and welcoming, [and] the partners especially go out of their way to make people comfortable."

Paychecks at Patterson Belknap lag after the first year, and associates have taken notice – but (amazingly) they don't mind much. (Even so, the firm tells us that the salary structure is currently under review.) Insiders say the tradeoff is a decent one: a smaller salary means less pressure. "Although Patterson Belknap pays less than other firms as you progress beyond the first year, the idea is that you don't put in the hours of the firms where the associates are getting $50,000 or so more than you," says a sensible Patterson associate. Indeed, insiders rave about the reasonable hours. "We have a target of 1,850 billable hours, but nothing rides on it – i.e., you still get your bonus if you're below 1,850," reports one contact. "People do not feel compelled to bill as much as possible here, and billing competition is all but nonexistent." Still, some say that the 1,850 number is not quite accurate. "Expected hours hover around 1,900-2,100 – not the 'official' target of 1,850, though many work less," reports one attorney.

Training is one area where Patterson Belknap may be behind the curve. "We need to improve here, and we are doing so," says a source. "When I came into the firm, there was almost no formal training, and that has changed," says that source, who adds that the new training "doesn't extend far enough into our associate careers." Learning as you go is common. "There is a lot more hands-on training at Patterson than at other firms," says an attorney. "For example, associates start taking depositions within their first or second year. By the fourth or fifth year, depositions are old hat."

Paul, Hastings, Janofsky & Walker LLP

75 East 55th Street
First Floor
New York, NY 10022
Phone: (212) 318-6000
www.paulhastings.com

LOCATIONS

Atlanta, GA • Los Angeles, CA • New York, NY • Orange County, CA • San Diego, CA • San Francisco, CA • Stamford, CT • Washington, DC • Beijing • Hong Kong • London • Shanghai • Tokyo

THE STATS

No. of attorneys firm-wide: 870
No. of attorneys in New York: 202
No. of offices: 13
Summer associate offers firm-wide: 66 out of 73 (2003)
Summer associate offers in New York: 16 out of 18 (2003)
Firm Chair: Seth M. Zachary
Hiring Partner: Mary C. Dollarhide

UPPERS

• Respected real estate and labor practices, growing in corporate and litigation
• Relaxed working environment

DOWNERS

• Increasing pressure to bill
• Many dissatisfied with bonuses

NOTABLE PERKS

• "Great gym package"
• Bagels and yogurt on Fridays, free cappuccino
• Emergency backup child care
• New associate training week

MAJOR DEPARTMENTS & PRACTICES

Corporate

Employment

Litigation

Real Estate

Tax

EMPLOYMENT CONTACT

Ms. Cindy Perrone

Attorney Recruiting and Development Manager

Phone: (212) 318-6898

E-mail: recruitNY@paulhastings.com

BASE SALARY

New York, NY

1st year: $125,000

2nd year: $135,000

3rd year: $150,000

Summer associate: $2,400/week

THE SCOOP

Founded in Los Angeles in 1951, Paul, Hastings, Janofsky & Walker has approximately 870 attorneys in 13 offices, including four in Asia and one in the UK. (A Shanghai office opened in 2003 and a new office is slated for Paris in 2004.) While the firm has historically specialized in labor and employment law, today its largest department is corporate, and it has strong litigation, real estate and tax departments, as well as growing M&A and finance practices. The New York office was established in 1986 and now has just over 200 attorneys. *New York Lawyer* ranked Paul Hastings No. 9 on its list of the top 25 New York offices of firms based outside the city. Legal publisher Chambers & Partners called the firm's real estate practice No. 1 in New York. The firm was also named M&A Law Firm of the Year by *Mergers & Acquisitions Advisor*.

Paul Hastings' real estate practice earned such praise with deals like the January 2003 sale of a partial interest in the Time Warner Center in Midtown Manhattan. The firm represented building owners Related Cos. and Apollo Real Estate Advisors in their sale of a 49.5 percent stake in the portions of the soon-to-be-finished building to MacFarlane Partners and the California Public Employees Retirement System.

The firm represented Inplane Photonics when the optical networking company raised $10 million in venture capital financing in March 2003. More recently, Paul Hastings' corporate practice represented investment bank SG Cowen Securities in its underwriting of the October 2003 common stock offering of Lions Gate Entertainment.

GETTING HIRED

Paul Hastings has no room for stiffs. "In hiring, I think the firm places a lot of emphasis on having a good personality," says one source. "I know people with excellent credentials who are rejected from Paul Hastings because they couldn't hold a conversation. I think the firm looks for balanced people." Industriousness is appreciated. "Paul Hastings looks for associates with a proven record of hard work and achievement," according to one insider. "While prestigious credentials are a plus, it is more important to demonstrate a commitment to working hard, completing projects and producing high-quality results."

OUR SURVEY SAYS

Paul Hastings associates agree that "the culture in the New York office is generally friendly," though some insiders suggest that "the firm culture is largely dictated by department." "By and large," says one source, "the real estate and litigation departments have a lot of camaraderie, a relatively laid-back culture and good partner-associate relationships. The same cannot be said of the corporate department, which is pretty uptight." Although several sources point out that "the firm culture is rather informal," social butterflies may be disappointed. "The lawyers here work hard during the day," explains an insider, "and do not spend much time together outside of work. It requires some effort to establish nonwork-related bonds with other lawyers."

Paul Hastings' hours requirements are typical of big New York firms. "Paul Hastings has a minimum annual billable requirement of 2,000 hours in most departments," says one insider, who goes on to say that the requirement is "equivalent to the minimum hourly requirement at most comparable firms." The firm points out that it generally expects associates to reach a target of 2,000 annual billable hours and that most associates record time within a range of 100 hours below to 200 hours above this target.

Just because the firm doesn't expect its associates to shoot for the moon doesn't mean there's no hours pressure at all. "The pressure to bill is omnipresent, but the partners have been really trying to calm associates' nerves about this issue," notes one source. "Regardless, it seems that job security is directly proportionate to one's billables." The pressure isn't just felt at yearly review time. "There is a tremendous focus on hours here – not only yearly but from month-to-month."

Bonus day can be an unhappy day for some at Paul Hastings. "Salary is competitive with other big firms in New York, but the bonus structure is not as generous as associates would like," reports one lawyer. Another insider agrees that the "bonus is a sticking point." And though some sources insist, in the words of one particularly descriptive lawyer, that the "discretionary bonus is about as elusive as a purple unicorn," the firm stresses that it has developed a plan to award discretionary bonuses to more associates, using such criteria as client service, participation in firm activities, community involvement, and quality and efficiency of legal work.

Paul, Weiss, Rifkind, Wharton & Garrison LLP

1285 Avenue of the Americas
New York, NY 10019
Phone: (212) 373-3000
www.paulweiss.com

LOCATIONS

New York, NY (HQ)
Washington, DC
Beijing
Hong Kong
London
Paris
Tokyo

THE STATS

No. of attorneys firm-wide: 523
No. of attorneys in New York: 428
No. of offices: 7
Summer associate offers firm-wide:
82 out of 82 (2003)
**Summer associate offers in New
York:** 79 out of 79 (2003)
Firm Chair: Alfred D. Youngwood
Hiring Attorney: Eric S. Goldstein

UPPERS

- High-quality work for prestigious clients
- Excellent M&A practice

DOWNERS

- Long hours
- Lower than expected bonuses

NOTABLE PERKS

- Friday cocktail parties
- Subsidized gym membership
- Free BlackBerrys
- Drawings for free theater tickets

MAJOR DEPARTMENTS & PRACTICES

Bankruptcy

Corporate

Employee Benefits & Executive Compensation

Entertainment

Environmental

Litigation

Personal Representation

Real Estate

Tax

EMPLOYMENT CONTACT

Ms. Patricia J. Morrissy
Legal Recruitment Director
Phone: (212) 373-2548
Fax: (212) 373-2205
E-mail: pmorrissy@paulweiss.com

BASE SALARY

New York, NY
1st year: $125,000
2nd year: $135,000
3rd year: $150,000
4th year: $170,000
5th year: $195,000
6th year: $210,000
7th year: $220,000
8th year: $235,000
Summer associate: $2,400/week

THE SCOOP

At Paul, Weiss, Rifkind, Wharton & Garrison LLP your options aren't limited but your liability is. The firm has over 120 years of experience in litigation and corporate matters (M&A is a strength) and is also well known for entertainment and individual representation.

The high quality of Paul Weiss' legal work inspires loyalty among firm clients. One long-time client is Time Warner. The firm represented Warner Communications when it merged with Time Inc. in 1989, then later managed the sale of a portion of TWE to AT&T. In 2002 Paul Weiss represented AOL Time Warner (now just Time Warner) in its quest to repurchase complete control of TWE. The firm's white-collar practice successfully defended Senator Robert Torricelli against charges of accepting illegal campaign contributions. (But it couldn't save Torricelli's 2002 Senate re-election campaign, which he abandoned after fallout from the scandal.)

In early 2003, Paul Weiss converted from a general partnership to a limited liability partnership. Several firms (including big names like Cravath, S&C and Cadwalader) have done so after being spooked by the lawsuits against accounting firms after auditing scandals at Enron and Tyco.

GETTING HIRED

Paul Weiss "operate[s] a very selective process, both at the screening and the call-back stages." In the words of a sixth-year associate, "Our standards are very high." While those high standards aren't a new thing, "the current economic environment has made hiring at Paul Weiss even more competitive." "Most of the associates here are from top-10 law schools, but the firm does hire associates from other schools." For candidates who have "the requisite academic qualifications, [the] interview process appears to be geared toward finding associates who have diverse interests and an interest in the law," according to a first-year.

A litigation attorney offers a different perspective, noting, "The whole process is somewhat random and depends on how candidates 'click' with their interviewers." A fourth-year advises that during the interviews, candidates should "make friends with the partners. Associate reviews are appreciated, but they do not seem to be determinative."

OUR SURVEY SAYS

Insiders say the firm's New York office is the type of place where "lawyers socialize and genuinely like each other." According to one midlevel attorney, Paul Weiss "has an eclectic, individualistic culture that can be at turns laid-back, friendly or uptight." "Everyone – from partners to secretaries – is on a first-name basis. It is rare to see closed office doors," reports one insider. Co-workers are "hardworking but down to earth," and there are "no excessive formalities" among attorneys.

On the whole, Paul Weiss associates are not very pleased by the number of hours they work, and many report difficulty balancing their work and personal lives. That said, insiders believe "the hours here are comparable to other big New York firms." "At times, I am unsatisfied with my life because of the number of hours that I am working. I think, however, that if I am going to be working these kinds of hours, I am happy that I am doing it here," reports a third-year. A second-year reports enjoying "the intensity of work and not being bored," but finds it difficult "to plan free time well, because I am constantly on call."

"We tend to stay with the pack" in terms of salary, a second-year tells us. While the salary is "appropriate," a first-year believes "the firm too often follows other major firms, despite being busier and more profitable." Insiders say, "Paul Weiss will never be the leader when it comes to compensation, but it always pays the market rate." There seems to be an undercurrent of "resentment that Paul Weiss could afford to pay higher bonuses," but did not. "We're obviously paid well compared to average folks, but are paid poorly compared to the hours we work and the firm's profitability. Bonuses have fallen over the past two years despite record profits." One annoyed associate boldly states, "As for bonuses, I think the partners were rather cheap, considering that they kept saying all year that we were turning away business and that they were having a banner year." Of course, there are also attorneys who are pleased with their salaries and think "the firm is great about keeping up with the market." "I think we are pretty much in line with other comparable New York firms," says a litigation associate.

Pillsbury Winthrop LLP

One Battery Park Plaza
New York, NY 10004
Phone: (212) 858-1000
www.pillsburywinthrop.com

LOCATIONS

Century City, CA • Costa Mesa,
CA • Houston, TX • Los Angeles,
CA • New York, NY • North
County San Diego, CA • Palo Alto,
CA • Sacramento, CA • San Diego,
CA • San Francisco, CA •
Stamford, CT • Tysons Corner, VA
• Washington, DC • London •
Singapore • Sydney • Tokyo

THE STATS

No. of attorneys firm-wide: 750
No. of attorneys in New York: 158
No. of offices: 17
**Summer associate offers in New
York:** 10 out of 12 (2003)
Chairwoman: Mary B. Cranston
Managing Partner: Marina Park
Hiring Partners: David Crichlow,
Courtney Lynch

UPPERS

- Special compensation system for
  senior associates
- International finance expertise

DOWNERS

- Culture in flux after merger,
  recession
- Little respect for associates' time

NOTABLE PERKS

- Bar expenses
- Six-week new baby leave (for
  women and men)
- Subsidized BlackBerrys and health
  club memberships
- On-site yoga

MAJOR DEPARTMENTS & PRACTICES

Antitrust

Bankruptcy & Creditors' Rights

Corporate, Securities & Finance

Class Actions

E-Commerce & Outsourcing

Emerging Companies

Employment & Labor

Executive Compensation & Benefits

Energy

Environment & Land Use

Intellectual Property

International Transactions

Licensing, Technology & Trade

Life Sciences & Technology

Litigation

Media & Content

Real Estate, Project Development & Construction

Tax

Telecommunications

EMPLOYMENT CONTACT

Ms. Dorrie Ciavatta

Director of Legal Employment

E-mail: dciavatta@pillsburywinthrop.com

BASE SALARY

New York

1st year: $125,000

2nd year: $135,000

3rd year: $150,000

4th year: $170,000

5th year: $190,000

6th-8th year: $195,000+

Summer associate: $2,404/week

THE SCOOP

The product of the 2001 merger between Pillsbury Madison & Sutro and Winthrop, Stimson, Putnam & Roberts, Pillsbury Winthrop boasts approximately 750 attorneys in 17 offices. With expertise in more than 40 areas, including securities and finance, technology, energy, telecommunications and litigation, the firm is perhaps best known for its international finance practice. Pillsubry was one of only three U.S. law firms in *Global Financial Review*'s 2003 ranking of top firms for international trade finance, coming in at No. 9.

Never one to be sidelined, especially in the face of an international opportunity, Pillsbury Winthrop created an Iraq reconstruction project team in July 2003. The team has 25 lawyers from across numerous practice areas and will advise companies bidding on projects or working with the new government in Iraq.

Pillsbury ended an ugly chapter in the firm's recent history and avoided a lawsuit by agreeing to a settlement with a former partner in April 2003. It all started in 2002 when Stamford, Conn.-based corporate partner Frode Jensen bolted the firm for competitor Latham & Watkins. Pillsbury took the unusual step of speaking out against Jensen after his departure, saying in a release that he had been accused of sexual harassment, that his productivity had slipped and that he was rarely in the office. Jensen filed a $45 million defamation suit after the release. The suit was settled in April 2003.

GETTING HIRED

No surprises in Pillsbury's recruiting process. "The firm is genuinely interested in finding people who fit in well with the group on a personality level," says one source. "But they expect top quality work, so you can't be a mental slouch." Insiders report the firm looks at Ivy Leagues first, but one contact worries the firm may "lose out on some hardworking, intelligent associates because they are so focused on Ivy League schools."

But the firm may be reevaluating its standards. "The firm is reconsidering what criteria it uses to hire associates since so many summer associates that come back permanently fail to work out," reports one associate. "The firm has much better luck with laterals and 3L associate hiring."

OUR SURVEY SAYS

According to our sources, the culture at Pillsbury Winthrop is still in flux after the firm's 2001 merger. "Pillsbury Winthrop used to have a very distinct and desirable culture," says one contact. "For the last couple of years, however, the firm has been in an identity crisis: wanting to be something it wasn't during the dot-com boom, and now attempting to retreat to what it was in its golden days." New Yorkers seem especially confused as to what the firm's vibe is nowadays. Says one Big Apple lawyer, "Formerly, the office had the laid-back attitude of a white-shoe law firm. Since the merger with Pillsbury and the onset of the recession, the atmosphere has grown more intense as expenses and productivity have come under constant scrutiny by firm management."

Hours are an issue. "Unfortunately, there is not enough work in the firm to go around," complains one contact. "So some 'choice' associates will have plenty of work, while others are told to be proactive about finding their own." Though the grass isn't always greener on the other side. "I find myself billing long days and weekends and still wondering if I am going to meet the firm's minimum expectations and my group's overall expectations," says a litigator. The biggest gripe is a lack of respect for associates' time. "Partners frequently walk into your office at 4:00 on a Friday with a weekend assignment," sighs one weary insider.

When it comes to the firm's recently revamped compensation system, associates disagree. Reports one source, "The 2,400-hour bonus was removed, and we now have guaranteed bonuses at 2,000 client billable hours, 2,100 billable hours and 2,250 billable hours. The difference between a 'client billable' and 'billable' is that billables include pro bono time, special projects and the like." Some explain that disposing of the hours-based bonus in the New York office leaves associates "with the impression that they will be making less money than their counterparts in the California offices." Associates like the "unique compensation component" that applies to senior associates. "Once you become a sixth-year associate, on top of your base salary, you receive point allocation much the same as the partners," explains one contact. "The firm believes in orienting senior associates to partnership, and this is one way to make you get a feel of what it is like being a partner."

New York associates are looking forward to leaving their "shopworn" digs behind and relocating to new space at 45th and Broadway. The new digs will feature state-of-the-art facilities and a more expansive meeting space, though one associate worries that "the space will be smaller."

Proskauer Rose LLP

1585 Broadway
New York, NY 10036
Phone: (212) 969-3000
www.proskauer.com

LOCATIONS

New York, NY (HQ)
Boca Raton, FL
Los Angeles, CA
Newark, NJ
Washington, DC
Paris

THE STATS

No. of attorneys firm-wide: 590
No. of attorneys in New York: 428
No. of offices: 6
Summer associate offers firm-wide:
58 out of 62 (2003)
**Summer associate offers in New
York:** 49 out of 49 (2003)
Chairman: Alan S. Jaffe
Hiring Attorney: Julie M. Allen

UPPERS

- Prestigious labor and employment, sports law groups
- It's fun to represent the rich and famous

DOWNERS

- Compensation lags for senior associates
- Retention issues for women and minorities

NOTABLE PERKS

- Department happy hours
- Professional back rubs
- The "world's greatest chocolate chip cookies"
- Firm-wide gala

MAJOR DEPARTMENTS & PRACTICES

Bankruptcy & Creditors' Rights
Corporate & Securities
Employee Benefits & ERISA
Entertainment, Sports & Intellectual
 Property
Estates, Wills, Trusts & Probate
Health
Labor & Employment
Litigation
Real Estate, Environmental &
Zoning
Tax

EMPLOYMENT CONTACT

Ms. Diane M. Kolnik
Manager of Legal Recruiting
Phone: (212) 969-5060
E-mail: dkolnik@proskauer.com

BASE SALARY

New York, NY
1st year: $125,000
2nd year: $135,000
3rd year: $150,000
4th year: $165,000
5th year: $185,000
6th year: $195,000
7th year: $205,000
8th year: $210,000
Summer associate: $2,404/week

THE SCOOP

At Proskauer Rose LLP, they've got their game faces on. The firm, which was founded in New York over 125 years ago by William Rose, is the legal representation of choice for a number of big-league sports clients, including Major League Baseball, the National Basketball Association and the National Hockey League. In addition to sports clients, the firm represents media and entertainment clients and has respected labor and employment, and bankruptcy practices.

Proskauer's ties to the sporting world go pretty deep. NBA commissioner David Stern is a former Proskauer attorney, as is NHL commissioner Gary Bettman. Thanks in part to Proskauer, Major League Baseball's 2002 collective bargaining negotiations were a smashing success: For the first time in 30 years, MLB and its players' union managed to avoid a work stoppage during labor negotiations.

The firm is defending Columbia University in a discrimination suit filed by a former employee in March 2003. The employee, formerly the acting director of the school's Office of Equal Opportunity and Affirmative Action, claims she was denied a promotion because she is an African-American woman and says the university has a pattern of discrimination.

In July 2003, Proskauer lured 20 litigation lawyers from litigation boutique Solomon Zauderer Ellenhorn Frischer & Sharp.

GETTING HIRED

Proskauer recruits at the top schools. But "there are a fair amount of associates who did not graduate from top-tier schools. A significant percentage, though not majority, of the partners are non-Ivy graduates." "Aside from the top national schools," reports a second-year, "we recruit among the top students at regional schools" including Fordham, Brooklyn, Seton Hall and Rutgers. The firm is looking for "smart people who can do the job but are still kind of down-to-earth – not necessarily the Type-A personality." A litigation attorney reveals that the firm is not only looking for "candidates who convey intelligence during the interview, but who [also] have engaging personalities." Don't forget to brush up on your people skills. "If you can't carry on a conversation, the firm does not want you regardless of what your grades are," warns a corporate attorney.

OUR SURVEY SAYS

Most associates report satisfaction with the laid-back culture of Proskauer, which one source calls "the anti-white-shoe firm." "The firm's culture is friendly, and while the firm is as big as other New York powerhouses, I do not think of it is as mean," says one associate. "The culture is generally quite friendly, but definitely has an air of formality to it as well," observes a contact. "The younger lawyers seem to socialize together on a fairly frequent basis, for a large law firm, anyway."

Though Proskauer Rose doesn't lag the market significantly, there're a couple of recurring complaints about compensation. "Our bonuses match the market but never make news," says a first-year. "[The firm is] on par with peer firms with respect to annual compensation for first- through third-years," says a fourth-year associate. "At the fourth-year level, there is a $5,000 gap. With respect to fifth-years and beyond, I assume that gap continues. With respect to bonuses, it is tied to hours and they are generally at market for the first- through third-year classes."

Proskauer associates seem resigned to the fact that "when you come to a law firm like this one, you expect to work long hours." "We are considered 24/7 attorneys and always on call. I find that most senior attorneys and partners here are respectful of associates' need for downtime. But when push comes to shove, if you are needed, you work." We're told part-time arrangements are rare. "The part-time program is only for people with child care issues, and very few associates participate," says one lawyer. One lawyer who works full time says, "From what I hear, part time is never part time. I know associates who work part time, and all it basically means is that you have one day a week off."

Proskauer Rose attorneys report the typical big-firm diversity issues, though some feel the firm does better than most. "I think it could be better numbers-wise, but it doesn't seem nearly as bad compared to the situation at many other firms," says a source. "I would love to see more people of color here, but I believe the firm works hard to recruit in this area," says another contact. Insiders say the firm offers a welcoming environment for gays and lesbians. A gay associate in the New York office reveals, "This is a good place to be out."

Schulte Roth & Zabel LLP

919 Third Avenue
New York, NY 10022
Phone: (212) 756-2000
www.srz.com

LOCATIONS

New York, NY (HQ)
London

THE STATS

No. of attorneys firm-wide: 337
No. of attorneys in New York: 330
No. of offices: 2
Summer associate offers in New York: 38 out of 38 (2003)
Executive Committee: Paul Roth, Martin Perschetz, Alan Waldenberg, Paul Weber, Marc Weingarten
Hiring Partners: Stephanie R. Breslow, Kurt F. Rosell

UPPERS

- Manageable hours
- Representing the rich and famous

DOWNERS

- Morale problem in IP
- Bonuses stable, even in the firm's "best year ever"

NOTABLE PERKS

- Alternative investment program
- Annual firm outing at Century Club
- BlackBerrys and laptops
- Gym discounts

MAJOR DEPARTMENTS & PRACTICES

Business Reorganization
Capital Markets
Employment & Employee Benefits
Environmental Law
Financial Services
Intellectual Property
Investment Management
Litigation
Mergers & Acquisitions
Real Estate
Structured Finance
Tax
Trusts & Estates

EMPLOYMENT CONTACT

Ms. Lisa Drew
Director of Recruiting
Fax: (212) 593-5955
E-mail: lisa.drew@srz.com

BASE SALARY

New York, NY
1st year: $125,000
2nd year: $135,000
3rd year: $150,000
4th year: $170,000
5th year: $190,000
6th year: $205,000
7th year: $220,000
8th year: $230,000
Summer associate: $2,403/week

THE SCOOP

Lawyers at Schulte Roth & Zabel LLP should be ready to rub elbows with some true blue bloods. The firm got its start representing hedge funds (complex, secretive and largely unregulated investment vehicles for very wealthy investors) and moved on to handling trusts and estates for the extremely well-heeled – think Rockefeller, Charles Lazarus (founder of the Toys 'R Us chain) and George Soros. Schulte Roth also handles corporate and securities, litigation, tax, employment and intellectual property matters.

Schulte Roth was founded in 1969 by seven partners to cater to the burgeoning hedge fund industry. The firm has grown gradually, but until September 2002 it was something of an anomaly in the legal profession: a big-name firm with only one office. That changed with the opening of a London outpost to cater to U.K. and European-based hedge funds.

Representing the rich and famous includes playing a part in public squabbles. Schulte Roth name partner William Zabel was in just such a drama; in early 2002 he was hired to represent Jane Welch, wife of former General Electric chairman and CEO Jack Welch, in divorce proceedings. The divorce proceedings caused a stir even beyond the usual attraction of big-name breakups. The two sides also clashed about the size of the Welch fortune, with estimates ranging from $450 million (from Jack's lawyers) to $800 million (from Jane's). The case was ultimately settled before trial in July 2003. Terms were not disclosed.

GETTING HIRED

It takes more than academic achievement to make it at Schulte Roth. "It seems to me that 90 percent of the associates that interview at big firms are scholastically qualified for the positions," observes one insider. "So it's that something extra that makes a candidate perfect for Schulte Roth. Because the firm has a social and friendly atmosphere, personality really counts." The firm is looking for more than Ivy League drones. "As a large New York firm, this firm seeks candidates from top-tier law schools who have excellent credentials," says one source. "However, I think the recruiting committee takes time to really get to know candidates and take into account their personalities and what they can add to the firm. This is not the type of place that hires only people from the Ivy League."

OUR SURVEY SAYS

Some Schulte Roth insiders agree with the colleague who says, "One of the best things about this firm is the culture." That cheerful associate continues: "I think that it is very friendly and people tend to be friends out of the office. Some of my best friends work here." Another contact says, "People are generally friendly and respectful of each other and seem to genuinely enjoy one another." IP associates have a different take. "Over the firm as a whole, the associates are reasonably happy," says one source. "In the intellectual property group, the associates are uniformly furious with the lack of advance planning by the partners, the weekly catastrophes and 20-hour days required to clean them up, the overbearing workload, the lack of management support to provide resources to get the work done with anything other than associate labor."

"As a first-year, I think my hours are very good, especially for a large firm," says one contact, who acknowledges that it won't always be this way. "I am fully expecting my hours to get much more intense and I know that midlevel and senior associates normally have very long days." A more senior associate shares some complaints. "The hours are one of the worst things about working here," gripes that source. "I don't think that it would be any better or any worse at any other big firm in New York City, though. Large firms in general require you to work a lot of hours."

Normally, getting paid market rates is enough to make most associates happy. However, Schulte Roth lawyers have a legitimate gripe with getting paid what everyone else is. "Base compensation seems on par with other firms, but the firm recently screwed us big time on bonuses," says one peeved associate. "In a year where the firm made record profits, and we all worked record hours, the firm gave the same piddly bonuses as firms that had nowhere near the great year we did. Can they say, 'Screw you' any louder to the associates?" "As a junior associate, my skill level is compensated," says one lawyer. This source confides, "I think all associates were slightly displeased with the bonus structure this year, as the bonuses were lower than last year after the firm repeatedly boasted of having its best year ever." (The firm, however, points out that it is one of the few firms to give merit bonus to associates and insists it paid market-rate bonuses in 2002.)

Seward & Kissel LLP

One Battery Park Plaza
New York, NY 10004
Phone: (212) 574-1200
www.sewkis.com

LOCATIONS

New York, NY (HQ)
Washington, DC

THE STATS

No. of attorneys firm-wide: 130
No. of attorneys in New York: 119
No. of offices: 2
Summer associate offers firm-wide:
10 out of 11 (2003)
**Summer associate offers in New
York:** 10 out of 11 (2003)
Managing Partner: John Tavss

UPPERS

- Super-friendly culture
- "Entirely reasonable" hours

DOWNERS

- Fewer perks than most big firms
- Training can be scarce

NOTABLE PERKS

- Annual country club outing
- Yearly formal holiday party ("the prom")
- Free sports tickets

MAJOR DEPARTMENTS & PRACTICES

Corporate Finance & Capital
Markets
Investment Management
Litigation
Real Estate
Tax & Employment Benefits
Trusts & Estates
Legislative & Regulatory
  Representation

EMPLOYMENT CONTACT

Ms. Royce L. Wain, Esq.
Director of Legal Recruiting &
Marketing
Phone: (212) 574-1684
E-mail: wain@sewkis.com

BASE SALARY

New York, NY
1st year: $125,000
2nd year: $135,000
3rd year: $150,000
4th year: $165,000

THE SCOOP

Seward & Kissel may lack size, but it makes up for it with expertise. The firm, founded in 1890 in New York, has approximately 120 attorneys in two offices – in New York and Washington, D.C. – with respected practices in seven areas: corporate finance and capital markets, investment management, litigation, real estate, tax and employee benefits, trusts and estates, and legislative and regulatory representation. The firm is one of the top legal advisers to hedge funds and their investors. In fact, CogentHedge.com, a hedge fund news site, named Seward & Kissel the top hedge fund law firm in a survey published in October 2003.

In addition to advising investors on dry land, Seward & Kissel is one of the top firms for naval and maritime law. Partners Larry Rutkowski and Gary Wolfe were named two of the top attorneys for shipping finance law by legal publisher Chambers & Partners. Moreover, Seward & Kissel was listed as one of the top three leading firms in shipping law and was described as having "substantial expertise in financing and transactional matters." The firm regularly handles maritime litigation in federal and state courts, as well as mediations and arbitrations before such bodies as the Society of Maritime Arbitrators.

GETTING HIRED

Seward & Kissel recruits at law schools across the country to fill its yearly quota of a dozen full-time associates and a dozen summer associates. The firm's target schools range from top-tier institutions like Columbia, Michigan and NYU to regional powers like Fordham, the University of North Carolina and Brooklyn Law. While grades matters, so too does personality and fit with the firm's culture. "Seward & Kissel is not a large firm," reports one insider. "Therefore, the firm does not mass hire. Furthermore, because the firm is small they look not only at a prospective candidate's credentials but also at how well the candidate will relate to co-workers." "I went through the early interview process and was hired," says another contact. "I did not find it any more or less stressful than interviewing with any other firm. In general, the firm is selective about new hires. Good fit appears to be important to the firm."

OUR SURVEY SAYS

According to firm insiders, the livin' is easy at Seward & Kissel, a firm with a culture that one source calls "very, very, very friendly." Another associate elaborates: "While the work is serious, there is not a feeling of cutthroat competition." "In the time I have been here, I have generally had at least cordial relationships with my colleagues, and, in some cases, have become close friends with colleagues. The partners are generally accessible. There is not a greedy feel to the partnership. There are no screamers – it's just not part of the Seward & Kissel culture." However, stubborn traces of formality remain. "The firm is laid-back and has gone casual," observes one attorney.

Associates at Seward & Kissel don't feel the same billable hours pressure that many of their counterparts at many other top firms feel. "You can work very, very hard, but the firm is not highly focused on billing X hours each month," reports one insider. Another contact notes, "Hours appear to be tracked, but I have never been pressured to bill a certain number. I've always had enough work to ensure that my billing is solid. Compared to colleagues at other firms, I find my hours to be entirely reasonable."

When it comes to compensation, associates are satisfied – though bonuses make some grumble. The firm "pays market, which is great considering the size of the firm and hours worked. However, bonuses are linked to hours, so many don't qualify." Still, Seward & Kissel can't be beat for smaller-sized firms. "The salary seems to be slightly above par for firms in its size [range]," says one source. Some find reason to complain when the subject turns to perks. "Because the firm is smaller, an associate will miss some of the luxurious perks that much larger firms offer," complains one lawyer.

Insiders warn that training is "left to associates, so you can get lucky or unlucky." When you get lucky, you get really lucky. "I have been involved in all aspects of litigation from the time I started here," says a senior associate. "Compared to colleagues at other firms, I have a greater skill set and broader range of experiences."

Shearman & Sterling

599 Lexington Avenue
New York, NY 10022
Phone: (212) 848-4000
www.shearman.com

LOCATIONS

New York, NY (HQ)
Menlo Park, CA • San Francisco,
CA • Washington, DC • Abu Dhabi
• Beijing • Brussels • Dusseldorf •
Frankfurt • Hong Kong • London •
Mannheim • Munich • Paris • Rome
• São Paulo • Singapore • Tokyo •
Toronto

THE STATS

No. of attorneys firm-wide:
1,000+
No. of attorneys in New York: 559
No. of offices: 19
Summer associate offers firm-wide:
79 out of 79 (2003)
**Summer associate offers in New
York:** 62 out of 62 (2003)
Senior Partner: David W. Heleniak
Hiring Partner: T. Robert Zochowski
Jr.

UPPERS

- Challenging international work
- Excellent commitment to pro bono
  work

DOWNERS

- Morale still low after 2001 layoffs
- "All or nothing" hours

NOTABLE PERKS

- Fourth-year retention bonuses
- Skybox at Madison Square Garden
- Posh dining room
- Rotations at international offices

MAJOR DEPARTMENTS & PRACTICES

Antitrust
Asset Management
Bank Finance
Bankruptcy & Reorganization
Capital Markets
Executive Compensation & Employee
  Benefits
Leasing
Litigation
Mergers & Acquisitions
Private Clients
Project Development & Finance
Property
Securitization & Derivatives
Tax

EMPLOYMENT CONTACT

Ms. Suzanne Ryan
Manager, Professional Recruiting
Phone: (212) 848-4592
Fax: (212) 848-7179
E-mail: sryan@shearman.com

BASE SALARY

New York, NY
1st year: $125,000
2nd year: $135,000
3rd year: $150,000
4th year: $165,000
Summer associate: $2,538/week

THE SCOOP

Founded in 1873, Shearman & Sterling employs more than 1,000 lawyers practicing in 19 outposts worldwide. Shearman's greatest strength is international corporate work, especially M&A. The firm's reputation took a hit after it laid off approximately 80 associates in 2001, but it has worked on rebuilding its reputation.

Shearman's project finance group is on a roll. In June 2002, the firm was named "Project Finance International Law Firm of the Year" by Chambers Global, then snagged *The Lawyer* magazine's "Projects/PFI Team of the Year" award less than a week later. In February 2003, three separate magazines singled the firm's project finance group out for praise, with two of the awards citing Shearman's work on financing the new Wembley Stadium in England and an integrated petrochemical facility in Nanjing.

In August 2002, Shearman represented Nelson Doubleday when he sold his half of the New York Mets to co-owner Fred Wilpon for a reported $131 million. Shearman lawyers have also pitched in to advocate for victims of the September 11 terrorist attacks. Attorneys at the firm successfully represented Marmily Cabrera, who was originally denied survivor's benefits because the federal victim's compensation fund did not recognize her common-law marriage, and the parents of Cantor Fitzgerald employee John Willett, whose landlord refused to return the deposit on the lease he had signed the night before he died.

GETTING HIRED

Shearman is looking for "smart, personable, independent starters" and "hardworkers." Insiders reveal that "exceptional international experience" or foreign language skills will land you in good stead, as will a "double background" of, say, an MBA to go along with your JD. The firm is "always desperate for Harvard, Yale and Stanford students," reports one insider. "Just hit the middle of the pack in any top-10 law school," advises one senior associate, "and Shearman will be a safety firm." A second-year corporate attorney insists, "We are all very book smart, with more than respectable academic credentials." The competition can be fierce: "Shearman remains a prestigious firm and draws ambitious, talented people."

OUR SURVEY SAYS

Shearman's offices may have a "veneer of gentility," but "an air of suspicion still pervades" after the 2001 layoffs. "The firm needs to find ways to convince associates that there is a strong future ahead for the firm and for their careers," states one junior associate. "Many associates continue to worry that they will either be let go if the economy doesn't improve or be overloaded with work if the economy rebounds," reports another. Though "many partners are great role models," the "clear *esprit de corps*" of earlier years "is now long gone."

It's often all or nothing when it comes to hours at Shearman & Sterling. "You either have nothing to do for weeks at a time or you're pulling 100-hour weeks," grouses a banking associate. "It's frustrating to have little to do during the day or during the week," complains another member of the banking practice, "and have new assignments on Friday afternoon to work on during the weekend on a regular basis." An attorney in the M&A practice group observes, "If you don't have enough work, you begin wondering when they are going to let you go." The subject of compensation, though, makes insiders smile. "The price is right," summarizes a second-year associate. Many junior and midlevel associates find, as one third-year corporate attorney reports, "Shearman's retention scheme, on top of bonuses, puts us ahead."

Despite the firm's "convenient location" and private dining room where attorneys can get "a four-course meal with linen service" on the cheap, few associates in New York have anything nice to say about their quarters. "The entire office is a dump," snaps one attorney, while another sighs, "The offices are an embarrassment." Others say the "ratty" décor is "stuck in the '70s," singling out the "sad lobby art" and "coffee-stained carpets." "Hopefully," a first-year litigator says, "our coming expansion to a new floor will cure some of the problems." (The firm confirms that it has begun a refurbishing project in response to the Manhattan associate complaints.)

With a full-time coordinator some associates describe as "arguably the best pro bono attorney in New York," S&S offers associates "numerous possibilities for pro bono work." At least in the New York office, "we've got more pro bono than we can handle" – everything "from hands-on litigation work and in-court representation to drafting constitutions and monitoring elections to advising international criminal tribunals."

Sidley Austin Brown & Wood LLP

787 Seventh Avenue
New York, NY 10019
Phone: (212) 839-5300
www.sidley.com

LOCATIONS

Chicago, IL • Dallas, TX • Los Angeles, CA • New York, NY • San Francisco, CA • Washington, DC • Beijing • Brussels • Geneva • Hong Kong • London • Shanghai • Singapore • Tokyo

THE STATS

No. of attorneys firm-wide: 1,596
No. of attorneys in New York: 441
No. of offices: 14
Summer associate offers firm-wide: 113 out of 117 (2003)
Summer associate offers in New York: 31 out of 31 (2003)
Firm-Wide Chairs: Tom Cole, Chuck Douglas
NY Co-Managing Partners: Joe Armbrust, George Petrow
Firm-Wide Hiring Partner: John Levi
NY Co-Hiring Partners: Rob Hardy, John Kuster

UPPERS

- Well-organized mentorship program
- Stable – no layoffs or pay cuts

DOWNERS

- Distribution of best work said to be uneven
- Bonus program "not competitive"

NOTABLE PERKS

- Emergency day care
- Subsidized train/bus passes
- Firm sports teams

MAJOR DEPARTMENTS & PRACTICES

Business & Banking Transactions
Corporate Reorganization &
  Bankruptcy
Corporate/Securities
Employee Benefits
Employment & Labor
Environmental
Food & Drug
Insurance
Intellectual Property
Litigation
Pooled Investments
Public Finance
Real Estate
Securitization
Tax
Trusts & Estates

EMPLOYMENT CONTACTS

Ms. Shana Kassoff
Legal Recruiting Manager
Phone: (212) 839-8600
Fax: (212) 839-5599
E-mail: skassoff@sidley.com

BASE SALARY

New York, NY
1st year: $125,000
2nd year: $135,000
3rd year: $150,000
4th year: $165,000
5th year: $185,000
6th year: $200,000
7th year: $210,000
Summer associate: $2,400/week

THE SCOOP

Sidley Austin Brown & Wood, formed by a 2001 merger between Chicago-based Sidley & Austin and New York-based Brown & Wood, employs over 1,500 lawyers in 14 offices in the U.S., Europe and Asia, including a brand-new office opened in Brussels in August 2003. The legal giant specializes in corporate, litigation, antitrust, bankruptcy, securities and tax law. Sidley's New York office has more than 400 lawyers and boasts clients such as global financial institutions, private equity funds, Fortune 500 companies, accounting firms, sports franchises, entertainment companies, real estate developers and pharmaceutical companies.

Sidley's litigation department in the New York office recently won favorable rulings for clients Merrill Lynch and Woori Bank and obtained a significant victory on behalf of Nomura Asset Management U.S.A. in an arbitration before the New York Stock Exchange. The corporate department recently represented Magna International in its spinoff of MI Developments to its shareholders, a transaction worth approximately $1.1 billion. And the New York office, along with lawyers from the London office, recently advised the investment banking arm of Deutsche Bank AG in a $2 billion London Stock Exchange-listed offering on behalf of Cadbury Schweppes.

In 2002, Sidley was ranked by Thomson Financial as top issuer's and top underwriter's counsel for U.S. debt, equity and equity-related deals and named the No. 1 U.S. law firm for overall client service by BTI Consulting.

GETTING HIRED

In Sidley's New York office, "the call-back interview consists of meeting with three attorneys for 25-minute interviews, two of which are usually partners. After the interviews, two junior associates take the candidate to lunch." Insiders say the firm is highly selective, recruiting from only a few choice schools. "If you are not from one of the top 10 to 15 schools, you will probably need to be on law review to get a call back." (The firm counters that it recruits from over 30 schools across the country.) A senior associate who helps interview candidates says, "I personally look for someone who is interesting to talk to and with whom I would enjoy working." Sidley "has a fairly firm grade cutoff, but there is some flexibility" if a candidate brings "other outstanding achievements" to the table.

OUR SURVEY SAYS

Sidley insiders in New York are of two minds. Some sources describe the firm's vibe as "very laid-back and friendly" and insist "the people are very friendly and supportive of each other" and the culture is "pleasant." Other insiders tell us attorneys are still adjusting to the firm's 2001 merger, and, as such, the culture is in flux. "The firm used to be a lifestyle firm, but that has long since passed. While the associates and partners are all still friendly, there is definitely a more uptight feeling," reports a junior associate. "The cultural divisions are still evident. [It's] hard to know when and how the two cultures will coalesce."

Most Sidley insiders believe the compensation at their firm is "competitive." Some even brag, "Sidley is at the top of the market." However, the sentiment that "bonuses are below market" was voiced by a number of associates. A corporate attorney explains, "The bonus is connected to billable hours, and as a result, many people get nothing!" (The firm insists that salary and bonus are commensurate with the market.)

A midlevel who considers her hours to be "pretty reasonable" says, "It can be hard to get enough billable hours. There has been more of a push in recent months to get the average hours up in the office." Other associates report that it's "difficult to manage the fluctuations in workload," and say they'd "gladly accept less pay for fewer hours." Hours can "fluctuate substantially between groups." A junior litigation attorney reports working "about nine hours or more a day" and "five to seven hours a weekend." "Sidley has been tremendous in giving me the opportunity to work from home at odd hours that allow me to spend more time with my young children," reports a very satisfied associate.

Although some associates report that "opportunities for training are very frequent" at Sidley, other insiders can't muster much enthusiasm for the training they receive. "There is a litigation training program at our office, and I think that corporate people have training opportunities. But that's about it" for in-house, formal training, explains a midlevel. "Training is pretty good for junior associates but is sparse for midlevel or senior associates." (The firm points out that it has added more training programs over the past year and routinely encourages its attorneys to attend outside training courses.)

Simpson Thacher & Bartlett

425 Lexington Avenue
New York, NY 10017
Phone: (212) 455-2000
www.simpsonthacher.com

LOCATIONS

New York, NY (HQ)
Los Angeles, CA
Palo Alto, CA
Hong Kong
London
Tokyo

THE STATS

No. of attorneys firm-wide: 681
No. of attorneys in New York: 635
No. of offices: 6
Summer associate offers firm-wide:
65 out of 65 (2003)
Summer associate offers in New York: 59 out of 59 (2003)
Chairman: Richard I. Beattie
Hiring Partners: Paul Curnin, John Carr, Marissa Wesely

UPPERS

- Serious prestige
- "Almost fanatical" commitment to pro bono work

DOWNERS

- Lack of communication between partners and associates
- Overcrowding in New York office

NOTABLE PERKS

- Car rides home
- "The world's best cookies"
- Free Starbucks coffee
- Services of real estate attorney for home purchase

MAJOR DEPARTMENTS & PRACTICES

Bankruptcy
Corporate (M&A, Private Equity,
  Securities, Banking and Project
  Finance)
Executive Compensation & Benefits
Exempt Organizations
Intellectual Property
Litigation
Personal Planning
Real Estate
Tax

EMPLOYMENT CONTACT

Ms. Dee Pifer
Director of Legal Employment
Phone: (212) 455-2687
Fax: (212) 455-2502
E-mail: dpifer@stblaw.com

BASE SALARY

New York, NY
1st year: $125,000
2nd year: $135,000
3rd year: $150,000
4th year: $170,000
5th year: $190,000
6th year: $205,000
7th year: $220,000
8th year: $235,000
Summer associate: $2,404/week

THE SCOOP

Founded in 1884 by three Columbia Law School grads, Simpson Thacher & Bartlett is one of the oldest and most revered of the Wall Street firms. With expertise in complex litigation, mergers and acquisitions, corporate governance, banking and capital markets, and securities, the firm has established a reputation as one of the most sought-after corporate advisors.

Simpson Thacher captured the No. 1 position on *Thomson Financial*'s ranking of firms completing the most M&A deals in 2002: 52 transactions totaling $193 billion. Thomson also ranked the firm at No. 1 worldwide for U.S. equity issuances. Simpson also grabbed the No.-8 spot on *Corporate Board Member*'s 2002 list of the top 20 firms corporations prefer to work with on national matters and tied for No. 20 on the magazine's list of the most admired firms. Additionally, Chambers & Partners ranked Simpson Thacher No. 2 in their survey of New York's top 10 firms and No. 1 in several practice areas.

The firm has the largest litigation department in New York and is the principal outside counsel to such prestigious clients as JPMorgan Chase, Accenture and Travelers. Simpson is currently representing Swiss Re in its high-profile courtroom battle against World Trade Center leaseholder Larry Silverstein and is acting as counsel to the independent board members of ImClone, which is at the center of the Sam Waksal/Martha Stewart insider trading scandal.

GETTING HIRED

"We are looking for top candidates" who "have something more to offer than a great resume," a third-year associate explains to would-be Simpsonites. A colleague in the litigation department concurs, explaining, "Great grades with a big ego, no personality or no life outside of school or work is not typically well received." Some, however, see things a bit differently. "Grades are key," says a midlevel, "which is a shame because being a good law school student does not necessarily translate into being a good lawyer." Insiders tell us that Simpson Thacher "seems to appreciate candidates with an uncommon background," especially those who "have done something else besides law." A New York associate confides, "The call-back interviews tend to be relaxed. I have the impression they are meant to establish if the candidate would fit in" at the firm because "law-related questions are rarely asked."

OUR SURVEY SAYS

"Simpson is an intriguing blend of fast-paced and cutting-edge legal work in an environment that retains a nice degree of civility," remarks a senior associate. Sources point out that Simpson is a "huge firm, so whoever you are, you can find your niche somewhere here." According to a litigation attorney, the culture at the firm is "extremely friendly and collegial – almost but not quite to the point of being laid-back." Others say the firm is "dignified," "traditional" and "appropriately formal."

Insiders report, "Although there does not tend to be much overall camaraderie between partners and associates, individual interactions are usually pleasant and can be rather friendly," and "for the most part, partners tend to value associates' opinions and contributions." "Like anything, it depends on who you work with," shrugs a noncommittal New Yorker. Another New Yorker confirms, "There are some great partners here," but adds, "for the most part, there is an 'us and them' mentality." Perhaps this is because "in some groups, junior associates work closely with partners, whereas in others – such as M&A – a fairly strict hierarchy is observed where junior associates might hardly ever meet the partner whose matter they are working on."

"Everyone wants to be paid more. I certainly do," admits an eighth-year associate. "But Simpson matches the top compensation of other big law firms, so you basically can't do any better." A second-year associate wisecracks, "We are paid well enough to have a very nice lifestyle – if we could get out of the office, that is." Many associates give the firm credit for matching compensation given by other leading firms. But several complain that the firm is "more of a follower than a leader in the compensation area."

No doubt about it. Life as a Simpson Thacher attorney means putting in long hours. And we do mean long hours. As is typical of life at a high-powered firm, hours tend to be "cyclical" and "unpredictable." According to a real estate attorney, hours can "fluctuate a lot, from leaving at 6:30 p.m. to working all night." A junior litigation attorney describes hours as "a roller coaster. One month you are swamped, the next there is a lot of downtime. Overall, though, the hours are very fair." A colleague echoes that sentiment, saying, "Some weeks are crazy, others are manageable. It's the nature of litigation and being an attorney."

Skadden, Arps, Slate, Meagher & Flom LLP and Affiliates

4 Times Square
New York, NY 10036
Phone: (212) 735-3000
www.skadden.com

LOCATIONS

New York, NY (HQ)
Boston, MA • Chicago, IL •
Houston, TX • Los Angeles, CA •
Newark, NJ • Palo Alto, CA • San
Francisco, CA • Washington, DC •
Wilmington, DE • Beijing • Brussels
• Frankfurt • Hong Kong • London
• Moscow • Paris • Singapore •
Sydney • Tokyo • Toronto • Vienna

THE STATS

No. of attorneys firm-wide: 1,800
No. of attorneys in New York: 876
No. of offices: 22
Summer associate offers firm-wide:
190 out of 195 (2003)
**Summer associate offers in New
York:** 110 out of 114 (2003)
Managing Partner: Robert C.
Sheehan
Hiring Partner: Howard L. Ellin

UPPERS

- Great training opportunities and informal mentoring
- High-profile work

DOWNERS

- Long hours
- Screamers among the partnership

NOTABLE PERKS

- "Fantastic" gym with trainers & classes
- $3,000 one-time tech allowance and annual $1,000 allowances after 2nd year
- Generous dinner allowances
- Month-long sabbatical after five years at firm

MAJOR DEPARTMENTS & PRACTICES

Antitrust & European Union
Banking & Institutional Investing
Communications
Consumer Financial Services
  Enforcement & Litigation
Corporate Finance
Corporate Governance
Corporate Restructuring
Employee Benefits & Executive
  Compensation
Energy & Project Finance
Environmental
Government Affairs
Health Care
Insurance
Intellectual Property & Technology
International Trade
Internet & E-Commerce
Investment Management
Labor & Employment Law
Litigation, Alternative Dispute
  Resolution & International
Arbitration
Mass Torts & Insurance Litigation
Mergers & Acquisitions
Political Law
Privatizations
Public Finance
Real Estate
Sports
Structured Finance
Tax
Trusts & Estates
UCC & Secured Transactions
White-Collar Crime

EMPLOYMENT CONTACT

Ms. Carol Sprague
Director of Legal Hiring
Phone: (212) 735-3815
Fax: (917) 777-3815
E-mail: csprague@skadden.com

BASE SALARY

New York, NY
1st year: $140,000
2nd year: $150,000
3rd year: $170,000
4th year: $185,000
5th year: $200,000
6th year: $212,000
7th year: $220,000
8th year: $225,000
Summer associate: $2,400/week

THE SCOOP

Armed with 1,800 attorneys and 22 offices around the world, Skadden, Arps, Slate, Meagher & Flom has created one of the most respected full-service law firms around – not to mention the richest. Skadden excels in the areas of litigation and M&A, with an impressive reputation in bankruptcy and real estate law as well.

The firm's M&A prowess has been proven time and again in its work on major deals. January 2003 found the firm working on behalf of client DaimlerChrysler when former Chrysler investors filed a $13 billion suit against the auto giant. And Compaq Computer sought Skadden's help in its highly publicized $25 billion merger with Hewlett-Packard in 2002. The firm represented Citigroup in its acquisition of Sears, Roebuck & Co.'s $29 billion credit card receivables portfolio, for a $3 billion premium. And the firm represented AdvancePCS in its $12 billion merger with Caremark Rx; Biogen in its $7 billion merger with IDEC Pharmaceuticals; and Credit Suisse First Boston as financial advisor to Oracle in its $6.3 billion bid to acquire PeopleSoft as well as in the related financing of the proposed transaction.

These days, failing corporations mean big business, and Skadden has represented many such corporations as they undergo financial restructuring. The firm participated in the reorganization of British communications company NTL and will reportedly receive a $4 million reward for its efforts. The firm navigated retail giant Kmart through the rough waters of reorganization following its high-profile bankruptcy filing and represented US Airways in its Chapter 11 restructuring.

GETTING HIRED

"First and foremost," an associate advises, "a lawyer must be bright to be hired at Skadden. In addition, however, the person must be able to put the quality of the work product ahead of his or her desire for personal recognition." Grades matter, of course, but so do other things. "The partners seem to look past GPA and school to find interesting and bright people," a new litigator observes. "We have our share of Harvard alums, but several of the partners went to Northeastern-type schools as well." A senior attorney describes Skadden as "much more concerned with how and what you've done in school than where you went."

OUR SURVEY SAYS

Despite a reputation for a demanding and hard-driving atmosphere, Skadden insiders praise the vibe at their firm. "For a firm of Skadden's size and reputation," one senior attorney confesses, "the culture is very laid-back." The "friendly, honest, busy" attorneys at Skadden are "very informal," say insiders. "Even Joe Flom is just 'Joe.'" Most of the partners at Skadden are "reasonable and helpful," except for a handful of "glaring and notable exceptions." The litigation practice, for example, "has its share of screamers and ghosts – those partners who head the case you work on but you have never met."

The relationship is simple, says one litigator: "They pay us a ton of money, and in exchange we work hard on demand." The "intense" "roller-coaster ride" of a Skadden work schedule is "either crazy or dead," but the "unsurprisingly long" hours are commonly regarded as "a tradeoff for getting interesting, fast-paced deals." At least there's plenty of help available. "No one is interested in seeing you fall on your face," says one young associate, so Skadden offers junior associates ample training opportunities, "so much that it is a bit overwhelming at times." The firm is serious about attendance: "If you don't show up for a training program, you hear about it." Informal mentoring is still the training of choice for many associates. "The informal mentoring I receive as part of being on a deal team," says a sophomore associate, "is far better at teaching me the skills I need to develop to be successful."

According to several insiders, the firm "talks the talk about diversity, and seems to walk the walk – at least with respect to entry-level and lateral hiring." The firm gets especially high marks for its "open, comfortable" treatment of gay and lesbian attorneys; some New York associates call Skadden "the best in the city in this respect."

"People come here for the money," is one midlevel attorney's frank assessment, and Skadden doesn't disappoint. "Every associate at Skadden's peer firms thanks Skadden for locking in their bonuses in our base salary," one source boasts, while junior associates find the high base pay "a godsend in this fragile economy." Still, some senior associates suggest the firm "begins to lag behind" its competitors after the first few years, especially since it "slashed the pay raises" recently.

Stroock & Stroock & Lavan

180 Maiden Lane
New York, NY 10038-4982
Phone: (212) 806-5400
www.stroock.com

LOCATIONS

New York, NY (HQ)
Los Angeles, CA
Miami, FL

THE STATS

No. of attorneys firm-wide: 365
No. of attorneys in New York: 290
No. of offices: 3
Summer associate offers firm-wide:
28 out of 28 (2003)
**Summer associate offers in New
York:** 24 out of 24 (2003)
Managing Partner: Thomas E.
Heftler
Hiring Attorney: Ross F. Moskowitz

UPPERS

- Laid-back culture
- Relaxed hours requirement

DOWNERS

- Bonuses slightly below market, especially for junior associates
- Some bonus secrecy and confusion

NOTABLE PERKS

- Annual firm-wide retreat
- Bonuses for bringing in new business
- Budget for tech expenses
- Weekly attorney lunches

MAJOR DEPARTMENTS & PRACTICES

Commodities/Derivatives
Employment Law
Energy/Project Finance
Entertainment
ERISA & Employee Benefits
Financial Restructuring
Financial Services Litigation
Health Care
Insurance
Intellectual Property
Investment Management
Litigation
M&A & Joint Ventures
Personal Client Services
Real Estate
Securities
Structured Finance
Tax

EMPLOYMENT CONTACT

Ms. Diane A. Cohen
Director of Legal Personnel & Recruiting
Phone: (212) 806-5406
Fax: (212) 806-6006
E-mail: dcohen@stroock.com

BASE SALARY

New York, NY
1st year: $125,000
2nd year: $135,000
3rd year: $150,000
4th year: $170,000
5th year: $190,000
6th year: $205,000
7th year: $210,000
8th year: $215,000
Summer associate: $2,400/week

THE SCOOP

It's hard to forget a name like Stroock & Stroock & Lavan LLP. The New York-based firm that bears this name is a corporate law specialist, handling finance, bankruptcy, intellectual property and litigation. The firm's client list includes banks, insurers and technology companies. Stroock was founded in downtown Manhattan way back in 1876 with two attorneys, but has since grown to over 300 lawyers in three locations.

Stroock has an interesting mix of clients. The firm is currently representing a couple suing MTV and the Hard Rock Hotel after being filmed for a hidden-camera reality TV prank. Stroock is also counsel to the landlord for the Beverly Hills location of Saks Fifth Avenue who claims Saks has doctored its books to avoid paying extra rent due if the ritzy retailer goes over $20 million a year in sales.

In 2001 Stroock launched the Public Service Project, a program that handles asylum cases, criminal appeals, disability rights, domestic violence cases and community economic development. The firm also has a variety of programs to assist victims of the September 11 terrorist attacks, including initiatives to help small businesses and the Firehouse Adoption Program, where Stroock attorneys work with the families of fire, police and rescue personnel killed in the attacks. The small business initiative provides legal services to small business in the World Trade Center area. The Stroock Spirit of New York Fund provides direct financial assistance to those affected by September 11.

GETTING HIRED

The first step to getting hired at Stroock is attending the right law school. "The firm hires primarily from NYU, Fordham, Colombia and Penn, with a sprinkling from Georgetown, BU and Cornell," reports one insider. "They are looking for law review or close to it at Fordham and comparable schools," says one New Yorker. "If you went to a top-five school, you'll get hired with Bs. If you went to a second-tier school like Brooklyn or American, you had better be in the top 1 or 2 percent." (The firm says it's more like the top 10 percent.) The interviews themselves shouldn't be cause for panic. "If you get a call back, be yourself, because if you've made it that far, the attorney is just testing to see whether you would make a suitable workmate," advises one source. "A Stroock call back is not one that should strike fear in your heart."

OUR SURVEY SAYS

Most insiders agree that Stroock is a "nice place [with] nice people" and "perfectly reasonable, as law firms go." Naturally, the atmosphere can vary. "The culture depends on which practice group you work for," says a first-year attorney. "However, no matter which group, the associates are not competitive, the partners and senior associates provide constant feedback and with the exception of an emergency, the office is pretty laid-back and informal."

The base salary at Stroock is "consistent with other Biglaw firms," "particularly at more junior levels," insiders say. But "at more senior levels, base compensation is lower than at other firms and bonuses usually lag those paid at other firms." "Our bonuses, on average, will not match the top echelon firms," complains one associate. "Even though we get paid a lot as attorneys, Stroock does not pay very much in bonuses, especially to younger associates," warns one source. "The bonus system is very unclear, and even though it is based on merit, it seems to have more to do with favoritism." Others counter that "the firm has a percentage share bonus for work brought into the firm" and an "above average benefits package that includes a home office expense account, technology allowance, parental leave policy that includes men, life and disability insurance, free parking and year-end bonuses."

"Relative to other large firms, the hours at Stroock are very reasonable," reports one insider. "Billing 2,000 to 2,100 hours a year will permit you to advance, receive a very fair bonus and be well regarded in the firm." Partner expectations can affect your hours worked. "Some partners expect their associates to bill no less than 2,200 hours, while others are satisfied with 2,000. Although the firm may not state an absolute minimum, little or no bonuses are awarded to associates billing less than 2,000 hours."

When it comes to training, Stroock associates are, for the most part, content. "Stroock has an excellent training program," insists one first-year, while other Stroockers say they appreciate the "tons of CLEs" offered by the firm. Some sources point out that most training at their firm "is informal and of the sink-or-swim variety." "Associates help educate one another," says one insider, who goes on to describe the "formal partner mentoring program." (He also says, though, that "other associates are often a better mentoring source.") Some associates suggest that, though "the firm is making a real commitment to training for mid- and senior associates," junior associates could use a little more TLC in the training department.

Sullivan & Cromwell LLP

125 Broad Street
New York, NY 10004
Phone: (212) 558-4000
www.sullcrom.com

LOCATIONS

New York, NY (HQ)
Los Angeles, CA
Palo Alto, CA
Washington, DC
Beijing
Frankfurt
Hong Kong
London
Melbourne
Paris
Sydney
Tokyo

THE STATS

No. of attorneys firm-wide: 729
No. of attorneys in New York: 503
No. of offices: 12

UPPERS

- Front-page work and prestigious clients
- Compensation leader

DOWNERS

- Unpredictable hours
- Need to improve retention of women

NOTABLE PERKS

- Aeron desk chairs
- Subsidized gym memberships
- Free dinners and car rides home
- Cafeteria breakfast "is like a hotel brunch"

MAJOR DEPARTMENTS & PRACTICES

Commercial Real Estate
Corporate & Finance
E-Business & Technology
Estates & Personal
Executive Compensation & Benefits
Financial Institutions
Litigation
Mergers & Acquisitions
Project Finance
Tax

EMPLOYMENT CONTACT

Ms. Nicole Adams
Assistant Manager of Legal Recruiting
Phone: (212) 558-3518
Fax: (212) 558-3588
E-mail: adamsn@sullcrom.com

BASE SALARY

New York, NY
1st year: $125,000
2nd year: $135,000*
3rd year: $150,000*
4th year: $170,000*
5th year: $190,000*
6th year: $205,000*
7th year: $220,000*
8th year: $235,000*
Summer associate: $2,404/week

* Salary not confirmed by the firm.

THE SCOOP

One of the bluest of the blue bloods, Sullivan & Cromwell has been a New York legal power virtually since its founding in 1879. The firm had a hand in the creation of industrial titans like Edison General Electric (in 1882) and U.S. Steel (in 1901). S&C continues the tradition of representing big name clientele; the firm has stood by Microsoft since 1992, including handling the various antitrust suits brought against the software behemoth. The firm's securities practice is considered one of the best in the country.

S&C more than holds its own in the high-powered world of mergers and acquisitions, landing the No.-1 ranking in the 2002 M&A league tables. Its name also pops up frequently in the annual "Deals of the Year" roundup in *Institutional Investor* magazine. The firm participated in 2002's largest M&A transaction when it advised Pharmacia on a $60 billion acquisition by Pfizer. The firm's litigation group coordinated defense efforts for a group of investment banks hit with law suits accusing them of rigging many of the "hot" technology IPOs between 1998 and 2000. Almost every investment bank you can think of has been named as a defendant, including Goldman Sachs, Merrill Lynch, Credit Suisse First Boston and Morgan Stanley.

The firm's pro bono practice group gives associates the opportunity to spend a full year working on pro bono cases under partner supervision. In September 2002, two associates at the firm secured the release of Lazaro Burt, who was wrongly convicted of murder and imprisoned for 10 years, spending the equivalent of 1,800 billable hours on the case.

GETTING HIRED

S&C views itself as "the last of the meritocracies" and chooses associates accordingly. A senior associate lists four traits the ideal candidate possesses: "Analytical firepower, presentation skills, creativity in approach to problem-solving and an entrepreneurial instinct." Another veteran associate observes the firm is looking for "sensible, professional, confident people with good judgment and good interpersonal skills." When one associate says the firm "looks at grades, grades, grades and pedigree, in that order," he isn't kidding. "The majority of associates come from one of the top-10 schools," observes a second-year, who adds encouragingly, "S&C seems to like to recruit one or two top students from a large number of second-tier schools."

OUR SURVEY SAYS

Got a type-A personality? You might fit in well among the "cult of perfectionists" at S&C. But "once past the baggage that comes with working to such a high standard, the culture is fun and social and provides for a good community," says a midlevel associate. A freshman adds, "Outsiders often mistake professionalism for stuffiness or pompous formalism. In reality, virtually all attorneys here are down-to-earth people who are focused on doing a good job for the firm's clients."

S&C "is not a place that cares about hours or face time," says one senior associate. "What matters is that you're around when people need you and you don't disappear on a deal. The flip side is that if a client needs you, they need you. It doesn't matter that you haven't had a weekend off in three months, doesn't matter that your mother's in town for the first time in years." Another corporate attorney chides, "You shouldn't expect to work on front-page M&A deals if you aren't ready to commit long hours."

With its "unwritten policy to match the top-paying firms," S&C keeps its attorneys satisfied. "Bankers got fired," a corporate attorney gloats. "We got a bonus." In fact, "this year, S&C upped the bonus announced by other New York firms," confirming the widespread opinion that the firm "leads the pack on bonus and salary."

"[S&C chairman] Rodgin Cohen seems legitimately dedicated to improving the retention of women at the firm," says one first-year female litigator, but the firm still has "a long way to go," counters a senior female associate. Meanwhile, the firm indicates that three out of the four litigation partners announced in November 2002 are women; in addition, S&C named a woman to the eight-partner management committee in 2003.

New York attorneys are desperately in need of elbow room. A "space crunch" has kept junior associates cooped together for as long as two years. The wait for a single office, according to New Yorkers, is "growing." (The firm says that, by its calculations, the wait is now actually shrinking due to space reconfigurations.) The space itself is frequently mocked. "There's a reason Ja Rule filmed his video in front of the Cravath lobby and not ours," observes one associate.

Thacher Proffitt & Wood LLP

Two World Financial Center
New York, NY 10281
Phone: (212) 912-7400
www.thacherproffitt.com

LOCATIONS

New York, NY (HQ)
Summit, NJ
Washington, DC
White Plains, NY
Mexico City

THE STATS

No. of attorneys firm-wide: 205
No. of attorneys in New York: 159
No. of offices: 5
Summer associate offers firm-wide:
19 out of 19 (2003)
Summer associate offers in New York: 19 out of 19 (2003)
Managing Partner: Paul D. Tvetenstrand
Hiring Partner: Andrea N. Mandell

UPPERS

• Collegial culture
• Solid corporate practice

DOWNERS

• Increased emphasis on the bottom line
• Pay lags

NOTABLE PERKS

• Friday pizza parties
• Monthly scotch-tasting parties
• Occasional sports tickets
• BlackBerry pagers

MAJOR DEPARTMENTS & PRACTICES

Corporate & Financial Institutions
International
Litigation & Dispute Resolution
Real Estate
Structure Finance
Tax
Technology & Intellectual Property

EMPLOYMENT CONTACT

Ms. Sarah Cuozzo
Manager of Legal Recruiting
Phone: (212) 912-7710
E-mail: scuozzo@tpwlaw.com

BASE SALARY

New York, NY
1st year: $125,000
Summer associate: $4,807.69/twice monthly

THE SCOOP

For more than 150 years, Thacher Proffitt & Wood has been a fixture of the New York corporate and commercial legal market. Thacher Proffitt was founded in 1848 by a father-and-son legal team. Today, the firm has more than 200 lawyers in five offices, including one in Mexico City. The firm's specialties include corporate transactions, structured finance, real estate and litigation, and it is proud to have topped the 2003 league tables for structured finance deals and U.S. debt issuer representation.

Though virtually all of Thacher Proffitt's 155 years have been spent in the Wall Street area, the firm's New York operations were housed in Midtown Manhattan for two years after the tragic events of September 11. The firm was housed on three floors of the South Tower of the World Trade Center, but no employees were hurt in the terror attacks. After two years at temporary offices on 42nd Street, Thacher Proffitt came back downtown in September 2003, moving into office space in the World Financial Center complex near the World Trade Center site.

In addition to new offices, Thacher Proffitt got new leadership in 2003. The firm's partnership elected Paul Tvetenstrand chairman and managing partner in February, succeeding Jack Williams, who had held the post for 12 years. Tvetenstrand is a structured finance specialist and a graduate of Columbia Law School.

GETTING HIRED

As is typical of the legal industry, Thacher Proffitt tightens its standards for new hires as the renown of an applicant's school ebbs. According to sources, the firm accepts the top 5 percent from the mediocre schools, top 25 percent from the top-40 schools [and] the top 50 percent from the top 10 schools. Nerds need not apply. "Super intellectuals do not seem to fare well here," says one associate who adds that Thacher Proffitt lawyers "need a good sense of humor and [need to] be amiable to succeed." A swelled head will also get you dinged. "The firm doesn't want egomaniacs, which works out, because most of them don't want to work here," says one contact.

OUR SURVEY SAYS

While many associates think the firm "is a very friendly, open-door place," there are some critics of the Thacher Proffitt vibe. "I suspect Thacher Proffitt is among the friendlier places as far as larger law firms," says one insider, while a newbie appreciates that "first-years are immediately integrated on a substantive level and are given considerable responsibility upon demonstration of capability." Says a happy midlevel associate, "I am constantly challenged and have knowledgeable people available for consultation as needed." Some, though, are worried that the times are changin'. "The firm has undergone a colossal transformation over the last two years and, instead of being a remarkable lifestyle firm, has become completely focused on profitability," gripes one attorney. "The firm's culture is an inherent contradiction – the place wants to be a big firm and a small firm at the same time," says one insider. "It wants to be a lifestyle firm and still make as much money per person as possible."

Associates realize that "any competitive law firm is going to demand long hours from you" and aren't dismayed that "Thacher Proffitt is no different." "While the number of hours expected is not high relative to other Manhattan firms, the pressure to bill is undeniable," says one source. On the bright side, "face time does not exist at Thacher Proffitt," and associates are asked to "just get your work finished on time and properly."

The firm's compensation scheme is a source of lament and discontent. One attorney says that pay issues are "by far the biggest complaint amongst the associates" but points out that "partners have taken some steps in the past year to correct it though – e.g., moving a portion of the bonus into the base salary." But Big Apple attorneys still feel they're being shortchanged. "Thacher Proffitt has always paid relatively low compared to New York City large firms," sighs one attorney. "They say it is a lifestyle firm, but the problem is that we really do work as long hours as many other firms. The difference is the collegial atmosphere." Some insiders say the bonuses are "not competitive," and others point out that "after a few years here, the [base] pay is subtantially below market."

Despite the salary discontent, associates have mostly positive things to say about those holding the purse strings. The Thacher Proffitt partners are considered "*very* approachable" and "respectful." Yelling is said to be "not acceptable." Still, some insiders say, "Sometimes there is a fundamental lack of respect for the fact that we are all adults and should be treated that way."

Thelen Reid & Priest

875 Third Avenue
New York, NY 10022
Phone: (212) 603-2000
www.thelenreid.com

LOCATIONS

Los Angeles, CA
Morristown, NJ
New York, NY
San Francisco, CA
Silicon Valley, CA
Washington, DC

THE STATS

No. of attorneys firm-wide: 450
No. of attorneys in New York: 139
No. of offices: 6
Summer associate offers firm-wide:
24 out of 26 (2003)
**Summer associate offers in New
York:** 6 out of 7 (2003)
Chairman: Chairman: Thomas J.
Igoe Jr.
Hiring Partners: Sharon P.
Carlstedt, Walter J. Godlewski

UPPERS

- Low hours requirement
- Relaxed culture

DOWNERS

- Confusion about non-lock-step pay
  system
- Narrow focus

NOTABLE PERKS

- Bar exam expenses and
  reimbursement for bar associations
- Brand-new offices
- Dinner and transportation allowance

MAJOR DEPARTMENTS & PRACTICES

Business
Commercial Litigation
Construction & Government
Contracts
Government Affairs
Labor & Employment
Real Estate
Tax, Benefits, Trust & Estates

EMPLOYMENT CONTACTS

Ms. Diane Amato
Attorney Recruiting Manager
Phone: (212) 603-2000
Fax: (212) 541-1518
E-mail: damato@thelenreid.com

BASE SALARY

New York, NY
1st year: $125,000
2nd year: $125,000-$135,000
3rd year: $130,000-$150,000
4th year: $135,000-$165,000
5th year: $140,000-$185,000
6th year: $145,000-$195,000
7th year: $150,000-$205,000
8th year: $155,000-$210,000
9th year: $160,000-$215,000
Summer associate: $2,400/week

THE SCOOP

Two plus two equals one powerful law firm – with the emphasis on power. Thelen Reid & Priest LLP clients include utility and power companies. Thelen Reid was formed by the 1998 merger of Thelen, Marrin, Johnson & Bridges (founded in 1924) and Reid & Priest (founded in 1935). Richard Gary, chairman of Thelen, Marrin, Johnson & Bridges, was elected chairman of the new firm while Reid & Priest chairman Thomas Igoe, Jr., became vice chairman.

In March 2003, Thelen Reid's partnership elected Igoe the new chairman by the narrowest of margins – a single vote. The vote was seen as a referendum on the firm's future as the two candidates (Charles Birenbaum, a San Francisco labor and employment partner, was the unlucky loser) articulated different visions for the future of Thelen Reid. Igoe was seen as a conservative candidate seeking steady growth while Birenbaum wanted to actively seek new clients.

Thelen Reid attorneys in three locations are inhaling that new office smell. The firm took on the challenge of moving its New York, San Jose and Los Angeles offices within a two-week period in November 2002. Though the Moses-like mass exodus was a logistical headache for the firm's office managers, the new leases took advantage of a down real estate market and allow for potential expansion. The trilateral move cost the firm approximately $20 million.

GETTING HIRED

According to insiders, Thelen Reid has become more selective with age. "As the firm's profitability and reputation post-merger have evolved, the caliber of schools and candidates has evolved as well," says one attorney. "There is still a premium on a good fit, rather than swooning over a sterling resume or transcript." "Personality and a positive attitude are very important criteria in our selection process," suggests one insider. Be yourself. Says another insider, "The recruiting process and the summer associate program is taken very seriously. The firm looks for more than grades or a cardboard cutout. Some individuality is rewarded." Not everyone is thrilled with the focus on personality. "I think the firm should raise their academic and extracurricular criteria and focus less on gut feelings about people," opines one attorney.

OUR SURVEY SAYS

Thelen Reid's culture is relaxed, say insiders. "The firm is very laid-back culturally, while at the same time people take their work and responsibilities to their clients very seriously," says a source. Another associate says Thelen Reid is a "good mix of laid back, friendly and seriousness about work. The firm asks you to work hard, but does not sweat the small stuff like working from home once in a while, coming in a little late after a long day or an occasional lapse in dress policy." "One of the main reasons I chose this firm is because of the culture – for the most part, everyone is very friendly," says one happy camper. "Even the most intense attorneys are approachable and good natured." "The people and personalities here are almost without exception wonderful," reports one contact.

New York associates are mostly pleased with their new office space. The firm is housed in a "brand new building with state-of-art technological capabilities." There are some empty spaces. "The offices are smaller and there are a number of them which are empty," complains one New York associate.

Unlike most big firms, Thelen Reid isn't keeping its associates chained to a desk. "Thelen Reid is a place that seeks quality of work over quantity," says one insider. "The partners are very, very pleased if an associate bills 1,950. The average billable hours is generally below 1,900." "While there is some pressure to meet your hourly minimums, there is not much pressure to work astronomical hours," says one source. Young lawyers seem to have the most complaints. "I was surprised at how hard it is to find work as a first year," says one rookie. "I thought that the work would be waiting there for me. This is probably the biggest challenge, finding the work to make the billable-hour requirement. However, it seems clear that making your billables does not make or break your career here, at least initially."

"Compensation is done on a meritocratic basis," says one associate. "It seems to be very fair. The people who do the most and best work get paid the best. And those people who prefer to work less get paid less." But some are confused about the compensation system. "We had yearly reviews, and the reviewers didn't say a single word about why we got the raise we did," says one source.

Wachtell, Lipton, Rosen & Katz

51 West 52nd Street
New York, NY 10019-6150
Phone: (212) 403-1000
www.wlrk.com

LOCATION

New York, NY

THE STATS

No. of attorneys firm-wide: 193
No. of offices: 1
Summer associate offers: 20 out of 20 (2003)
Chairman: Richard D. Katcher
Hiring Partner: By committee

UPPERS

- Major prestige and whopping paychecks
- Loads of responsibility from the start

DOWNERS

- Little in the way of hand-holding
- "Long, difficult hours"

NOTABLE PERKS

- Top-notch technology at your disposal
- Fully stocked kitchen on each floor with kitchen staff
- In-house birthday parties for attorneys
- Fro-yo machine

MAJOR DEPARTMENTS & PRACTICE AREAS

Antitrust
Bankruptcy
Corporate
Creditors' Rights
Executive Compensation & Benefits
Litigation
Real Estate
Tax
Trust & Estates

EMPLOYMENT CONTACT

Ms. Elizabeth F. Breslow
Dir. of Recruiting and Legal Personnel
Phone: (212) 403-1334
Fax: (212) 403-2334
E-mail: recruiting@wlrk.com

BASE SALARY

New York, NY
1st year: $140,000
2nd year: $150,000
3rd year: $165,000
4th year: $180,000
5th year: $195,000
Summer associate: $2,404/week

THE SCOOP

Wachtell, Lipton, Rosen & Katz might be proof that size isn't everything. The firm has 193 lawyers in its sole office in the Big Apple, making it small in comparison to many of its competitors. But there's nothing small about Wachtell's reputation. The firm, which is known as a litigation and M&A powerhouse, pioneered one of the leading strategies for a company seeking to avoid a hostile takeover bid. In the 1980s, firm co-founder Martin Lipton invented the "poison pill" strategy where a company sells shares at a discounted price to current shareholders, making a takeover bid more costly.

Unlike many of its competitors, Wachtell specializes in just a few key practice areas; in addition to litigation and M&A, the firm excels at creditors' rights, real estate, tax, antitrust and executive compensation. Moreover, Wachtell does not work with clients on a retainer basis. Instead, the firm chooses to take on a client based on the merits of each particular case or deal. This out-of-the-box thinking has paid off: Not only do Wachtell attorneys command high fees, the firm's associates are the highest paid in the nation. Wachtell generally doesn't bill hourly rates as at most firms, but instead bases fees on a variety of factors, including the complexity of the deal and how well the firm handles the matter. Like investment bankers, the firm generally pockets a percentage of the value of the deals they negotiate.

Wachtell better spiff up its offices and start cooking up some goat cheese tartlets; Martha Stewart is coming to town. The firm is representing the domestic diva and media mogul in her insider trading trial.

GETTING HIRED

One freshman attorney describes Wachtell as the "hardest offer in [New York]." Another recalls, "My Wachtell interview was the most difficult of all of my interviews, but I was impressed that the attorneys were more interested in determining whether I was a good fit for the place than in recruiting me and selling the firm." Everybody agrees on what goes into that determination. "You absolutely must have excellent grades, period," says a third-year associate. "Personality can tank you in the interview, but even the best personality and intangibles will not get you a call back unless you have excellent, law review-caliber grades." "If you don't have stellar grades and law review, it will be almost impossible to get hired," a senior associate concurs, while another attorney chimes in, "Law journal work also appears essential if a candidate does not attend a top-three law school."

OUR SURVEY SAYS

Wachtell's "very intense" offices are "quiet but congenial" and "surprisingly informal," despite the relentlessly formal dress code. "People here genuinely like each other and there are many close friendships," enthuses a third-year associate, "but very little socializing together outside the office." A senior member of the corporate practice says firm pride "creates a friendly atmosphere. We're in it together, so why not be nice?"

"The collegiality between even the most senior partners and the most junior associates here continues to astonish me," a second-year marvels. Another associate avers, "You are treated as a colleague and a potential future partner from day one." "What matters most here," a bankruptcy attorney says, "is your dedication to consistently doing work of extraordinary quality. If you are good at what you do, you are valued, period."

"Nobody pretends that Wachtell is a lifestyle firm," but the long hours can be dismaying. "The life/work boundary should be more respected," suggests one rookie associate, "so there is no macho attitude about staying all night and working all weekend." Another first-year counters frankly, "Working at Wachtell will be your life. You just have to be prepared to accept that fact." Even a senior attorney complains, "I work way too many hours. More every year." But, says another associate, "I rarely feel that I'm spending my time doing things that are unnecessary." And a third-year associate says it's not so hard to find a balance. "I've rarely had to cancel plans unexpectedly, and never had to cancel a vacation," she offers. "You are deeply involved in, and informed about, your matters, so you can better plan your time outside the office."

Can you say ca-ching? Wachtell is "committed to paying a leading salary" and "consistently pays substantially more than anyplace else." Even in the current economic situation, associates describe the firm as "unbelievably" and "extraordinarily" generous, and call their salaries and bonuses "a major reason to come to this firm as opposed to the other top 10 firms in New York City." A senior associate proudly boasts, "I'm being paid better than contemporaries at other firms, and with my bonus, I'm making more than even partners at lots of firms." No wonder a midlevel litigator insists, "It makes no sense to work at another big New York firm, if you can work here."

Weil, Gotshal & Manges LLP

767 Fifth Avenue
New York, NY 10153
Phone: (212) 310-8000
www.weil.com

LOCATIONS

New York, NY (HQ)
Austin, TX
Boston, MA
Dallas, TX
Houston, TX
Miami, FL
Silicon Valley, CA
Washington, DC
Brussels
Budapest
Frankfurt
London
Paris
Prague
Singapore
Warsaw

THE STATS

No. of attorneys firm-wide: 1,075
No. of attorneys in New York: 565
No. of offices: 16
Summer associate offers firm-wide:
93 out of 95 (2003)
**Summer associate offers in New
York:** 68 out of 68 (2003)
Chairman: Stephen J. Dannhauser
Hiring Partners: Todd Chandler,
Helyn Goldstein, Josh Krevitt, Rod
Miller

UPPERS

- "Individuality is actually
  encouraged"
- Top bankruptcy practice

DOWNERS

- Dissolution of retention bonus is a
  sore spot
- Work allocation can be uneven

NOTABLE PERKS

- Technology stipend
- Monthly lottery for sports and
  concert tickets
- Four-week paid parental leave
- Firm and department retreats

MAJOR DEPARTMENTS & PRACTICE AREAS

Advertising
Antitrust/Competition Law
Business & Restructuring
Business & Securities Litigation
Capital Markets
Consumer Finance
Corporate
Criminal (White-Collar Crime)
First Amendment
Institutional Finance
Intellectual Property
Labor & Employment
Litigation & Arbitration
Media & Technology
Mergers & Acquisitions
Private Equity
Product Liability
Real Estate
Sports
Structured Finance & Derivatives
Tax
Trade Practices & Regulatory Law

EMPLOYMENT CONTACT

Ms. Donna J. Lang
Manager of Legal Recruiting
Fax: (212) 735-4502
E-mail: donna.lang@weil.com

BASE SALARY

New York, NY
1st year: $125,000
2nd year: $135,000
3rd year: $150,000
4th year: $165,000
5th year: $190,000
6th year: $205,000
7th year: $215,000
Summer associate: $2,400/wk

THE SCOOP

If you're going broke, most likely you're going to Weil, Gotshal & Manges. The firm has one of the most respected bankruptcy practices in the legal profession with a client list that's a Who's Who of bankrupt companies. Recent and prominent clients include Enron, WorldCom, Global Crossing, and Bethlehem Steel, plus major creditors of Kmart, US Air and United Airlines. Weil's preeminence in the restructuring and finance area has helped it prosper during the economic downturn while other firms have suffered.

But bankruptcy isn't the only game at Weil Gotshal. In fact, half of the firm's attorneys are in the corporate department, and the transaction side has been scoring at or near the top of the M&A league tables tracked by Bloomberg and Thompson for the past two years. Major corporate matters include multi-billion dollar deals for long-time client GE, as well as high-profile work for Vivendi, Hicks Muse Tate & Furst, and Tommy H. Lee, all of which frequently involve heavy use of the firm's international offices. More than one-third of the firm's attorneys are litigators, with significant muscle in IP, patent and securities litigation. The department serves blue chip clients such as ExxonMobil, Cisco, Intel, American Airlines and Disney.

In January 2003, the firm merged with Paris-based M&A boutique Serra Leavy & Cazals and began operating an office in the City of Lights under the Weil Gotshal name, adding to its existing European presence in London, Frankfurt, Brussels and Central Europe. Meanwhile, five attorneys migrated from the firm's Houston location to establish an Austin outpost in February 2003.

GETTING HIRED

"Weil seems to be increasingly selective. They're focusing more on grades and caliber of law school, while still looking for people who are smart – and not just book smart – accomplished and motivated," remarks an associate. The firm is said to value candidates who are "resourceful, analytical and confident and have good common sense." Additionally, it helps to have "a good and interesting personality." "If you're well organized with a can-do attitude, you can get hired here," observes one source. "Where you went to school and grades are less important here than at other top-20 firms." Not everyone concurs. "We are very grade-conscious, so it can be difficult for talented lawyers with midlevel academics to even get an in-office interview," an insider confides.

OUR SURVEY SAYS

"Weil Gotshal is really a meritocracy. So if you work hard, you will get ahead and you will be constantly challenged," a midlevel attorney asserts. "Weil will give you as much responsibility as you are willing to take on, which cannot be said of most other firms," says another contact. Others bemoan the "seriously inequitable distribution of work." A second-year explains, "If you show you are willing to work hard and you'll do a good job, you tend to get more and more work piled on, while other associates are leaving at 6 p.m. and don't appear to have much to do. I think this is an overall complaint that a lot of people have at different firms in the city."

"Our salaries are fantastic," says one Weil insider, "but the firm is incredibly cheap with bonuses, especially in light of how profitable WGM is." Others confirm the dissolution of the retention bonus is a sore spot among associates given the "great financial stability" of the firm. But many associates seem unfazed by the bonus situation. Weil pays "the same as other top New York firms," they tell us. "There have been some nickel-and-dime cuts due to the recession," admits a first-year, "but pay is still equal to or better than any firm I'm aware of." And a senior associate believes, "The compensation here is competitive with peer firms. There are very few firms that pay more."

Associates at Weil Gotshal have some intense feelings about the hours they keep. Even among those who say the hours are more "a product of big firm life rather than Weil itself," there are many who bemoan the long days. "Our hours are no better and no worse than any other firm. That said, I think you'd be hard pressed to find an associate who didn't want to have more free time," observes an IP attorney. "I work long hours, but because I like the work and the people, it is not an issue," says a first-year. A senior associate describes the hours as "very cyclical. Sometimes it's 15 hours a day, then it's back to eight to nine hours a day," depending on "what deals are going on." A bankruptcy attorney reports spending an "outrageous number of hours" working and "regularly billing 80 [hours] per week."

White & Case LLP

1155 Avenue of the Americas
New York, NY 10036-2787
Phone: (212) 819-8200
www.whitecase.com

LOCATIONS

New York, NY (HQ)
Los Angeles, CA
Miami, FL
Palo Alto, CA
San Francisco, CA
Washington, DC
+ 32 other offices worldwide

THE STATS

No. of attorneys firm-wide: 1,671
No. of attorneys in New York: 374
No. of offices: 38
Managing Partner: Duane D. Wall
Hiring Partner: M. Elaine Johnston

UPPERS

- Global reputation
- Pro bono stars

DOWNERS

- Mysterious bonus scheme
- Poor record on racial diversity

NOTABLE PERKS

- Free on-site gym
- Generous summer associate lunch budget
- Sports tickets and museum passes
- Summer parties at New York landmarks

MAJOR DEPARTMENTS & PRACTICES

Banking
Litigation/Intellectual Property
Mergers & Acquisitions
Projects/Leasing
Securities
Tax

EMPLOYMENT CONTACT

Ms. Dana E. Stephenson
Dir. of Attorney Recruiting & Employment
Phone: (212) 819-8200
Fax: (212) 354-8113
E-mail: recruit@whitecase.com

BASE SALARY

New York, NY
1st year: $125,000
2nd year: $135,000
3rd year: $150,000
4th year: $170,000
5th year: $190,000
6th year: $200,000
7th year: $205,000
8th year: $210,000
Summer associate: $2,403/week

THE SCOOP

Rising from humble beginnings, White & Case is now one of the few truly global law firms. The firm was founded in New York in 1901 and from the beginning represented big names like Bankers Trust and J.P. Morgan. White & Case now has over 1,600 attorneys in 38 offices around the world, and the firm's attorneys continue to represent prominent clients. For example, partner George J. Terwilliger III played an important role in the case of the century (last century, that is). Terwilliger was part of George W. Bush's legal team in Bush v. Gore, the challenge to the 2000 presidential election results in Florida.

Terwilliger isn't the firm's only member with political connections. In July 2003, James J. McGuire, formerly the top legal adviser to New York Governor George Pataki, joined White & Case as counsel in the firm's commercial litigation practice.

White & Case has renewed its commitment to pro bono law in recent years. The firm began its pro bono work during World War I by representing the Red Cross. James Stillwagon, head of the firm's corporate immigration practice, became full-time chair of the pro bono committee in May 2002, at a time when White & Case has rocketed to the top of pro bono rankings. The firm placed fourth in *The American Lawyer* pro bono rankings in 2002 and 2001. That's an improvement from the firm's ranking in 2000 (No. 7) and a major jump over 1999, when White & Case came in at No. 48.

GETTING HIRED

White & Case, like many of its peer firms, is more selective now than in years past, due in large part to the sluggish economy. "The firm has been getting very picky due to the economy, with a lot of emphasis on grades," reports one insider. "A lot also depends on the interview and your ability to impress people." According to one White & Case associate, the firm now primarily seeks "candidates from top-20 schools."

Those interested in White & Case should keep in mind the firm's international reach and should highlight their own international experience as much as possible. "Given the firm's international focus, language skills and time spent abroad or interests abroad are highly valued and make for a more diverse group of people than at most other firms," says one source.

OUR SURVEY SAYS

White & Case associates are divided on the firm's culture; some find the vibe more laid-back than nerve-racking, while others say the firm's drive to succeed gives lawyers an unfriendly edge. No matter what your experience, lay off the comedy. "Nobody seems to be able to tell when I am making a joke," says one would-be Carrot Top. "It's not that it's formal or stuffy here, it's just that nobody seems to expect a joke at any given time."

For the most part, White & Case attorneys are resigned to the long hours they log. "Hours are part of the bargain," sighs one insider. "Everyone knows it is not a nine-to-five job most days. That said, this is no sweatshop, and people are genuinely sensitive to the need to have a personal/family life." The unpredictability of their hours bugs many insiders. Says one associate, "What gets to you is the erratic nature of [the hours]. You spend 15 hours a day for a whole month, and then you have nothing to do for another month."

"Compensation is as good as at any big law firm," says one well-paid insider. "However, White & Case has a tendency to follow the others rather than being a leader. Especially on bonuses, they can be a bit cheap." The bonus structure is a source of confusion and complaint. "The 2,000-billable hours requirement in order to receive the bonus is too high," says one associate. "The firm has low-balled on bonuses each of the past three years and has attempted – and failed – to mislead associates about the details of the three successive schemes each year," fumes another contact.

Training is improving, according to insiders. "[Training] has historically been a massive problem at this firm," says a corporate lawyer. "However, it seems that there is an effort under way at the moment to improve this in the securities section." Big Apple lawyers have ample opportunity to learn. "The White & Case New York office provides over 200 on-site courses a year given by White & Case attorneys and outside providers," reports one insider.

The firm's record when it comes to minority recruiting and retention troubles some insiders. "The firm is committed to having a diverse group of associates," states one insider. "However, this diversity does not seem to extend to the partnership rank, especially in the New York office."

Willkie Farr & Gallagher

The Equitable Center
787 Seventh Avenue
New York, NY 10019-6099
Phone: (212) 728-8000
www.willkie.com

LOCATIONS

New York, NY (HQ)
Washington, DC
Brussels
Frankfurt
London
Milan
Paris
Rome

THE STATS

No. of attorneys firm-wide: 530
No. of attorneys in New York: 368
No. of offices: 8
Summer associate offers firm-wide:
61 out of 61 (2003)
**Summer associate offers in New
York:** 56 out of 56 (2003)
Chairman: Jack H. Nusbaum
Hiring Partners: Jeffrey R. Poss,
Thomas H. Golden, William Gump,
Loretta Ippolito, David Boston

UPPERS

- "As laid-back as it gets"
- No billable hours requirements

DOWNERS

- Over-market revenues, but mere
  market bonuses
- Unpredictable shifts in workload

NOTABLE PERKS

- Bagels every morning, cookies every
  afternoon
- Attorney lounge with flat-screen TV
  and DVD player
- Dinners and car rides after 8 p.m.
- Subsidized gym memberships

MAJOR DEPARTMENTS & PRACTICE AREAS

Bankruptcy
Corporate/Finance
Employee Benefits & Relations
Intellectual Property
Litigation
Real Estate
Tax
Trusts & Estates

EMPLOYMENT CONTACTS

Hiring Partners Thomas Golden,
Jeffrey Poss, Loretta Ippolito, William
Gump, and Dave Boston
Phone: (212) 728-8000

BASE SALARY

New York, NY
1st year: $125,000
2nd year: $135,000
3rd year: $150,000
4th year: $170,000
5th year: $190,000
Summer associate: $2,404/week

THE SCOOP

Willkie Farr & Gallagher, founded in New York in 1899, is known, in part, for its political connections. Name partner Wendell Willkie was the Republican nominee for president in 1940, and former New York governor Mario Cuomo joined the firm in 1995. Willkie Farr represents current New York City Mayor Michael Bloomberg and the media company he founded, Bloomberg L.P.

Recent times have seen European expansion for Willkie Farr. The firm opened offices in Frankfurt, Rome and Milan in 2000 and merged with Brussels-based Dieux & Associes in March 2002.

Willkie Farr serves as lead counsel to 17 nations accused of dumping their steel products on the American market at artificially low prices. And the firm represented the office of Major League Baseball's commissioner, successfully facing down the heavy hitters representing former owners of the Montreal Expos in a federal racketeering lawsuit. In the suit, the plaintiffs alleged that baseball commissioner Bud Selig and other league officials cooked up a scheme with one-time Expos general managing partner Jeffrey Loria to run the Expos franchise into the ground to force dissolution or relocation to a potentially more lucrative market. The suit against MLB was temporarily stayed in November 2002 when a judge ordered the plaintiffs to resolve their dispute with Loria before engaging other defendants.

GETTING HIRED

"If there is one quality they look for more than anything else" at Willkie Farr, says one recent hire, "it is good judgment, which will come through in social as well as work settings." Other associates stress the importance of social compatibility as well, saying "the firm puts an emphasis on personality as much as possible" and seeks out "people who will be fun on a social occasion, but who will take their work seriously." Says one second-year associate, "If you went to a top law school or a lower-tier school and were on law review or had top grades, getting hired is not a problem." A first-year advises, "Interviewers tell it like it is around here and are mostly trying to determine if you fit the mold."

OUR SURVEY SAYS

"As big New York law firms go," a second-year associate reports, "Willkie is as laid-back as it gets." The prevailing mood is "friendly and social but competitive." A midlevel litigator admits, "Sometimes, the urgency of the work can create an intense environment, but that is the exception, not the norm." "All my professional relationships and personal relationships are extremely positive," says an enthusiastic first-year. "My best friends are at the firm." But the "quirky" environment "can tend toward cliquishness" and, says a midlevel corporate attorney, echoing the observations of lawyers across the nation, "the atmosphere has been much less pleasant since the economy slowed down."

"Too much to do, too many hours, too many nights and weekends," sighs an IP associate. "But what do you expect for what they pay us?" Indeed, many Willkie-ers say their hours are just plain overwhelming. Some admit it could be worse. One source says his hours are better than many of his fellow associates at Willkie and other firms, but "the fact of the matter is that if something needs to get done and it needs to be done by Monday morning, you can expect to be here all weekend." A sophomore associate has "enough ownership over my projects that I can manage my schedule in such a way that I can get out of the office when I need to," and several associates confirm partners are "respectful of your time." ("Vacations are sacrosanct," confides an insider.)

Associates firm-wide agree their salaries are "consistent with other New York firms." But, adds one first-year, "sometimes to the detriment of associates." It seems that, after a self-declared year of record revenues, Willkie's partners "followed the market instead of granting higher bonuses." A second-year litigator comments, "Everyone outside large New York law firms cannot believe that associates would complain about their compensation. But the fact is the partners are still making many times what any of the associates make, and the associates kill themselves for the partners." A senior corporate attorney asks, "Why were bonuses less than the year before and not reflective of one of the greatest years at the firm? It is odd that the partners often forget who helps to earn the majority of the revenues."

APPENDIX

Psst...
Need a Change in Venue?

Use the Internet's most targeted
job search tools for law
professionals.

Vault Law Job Board

The most comprehensive and convenient job board for law
professionals. Target your search by area of law, function,
and experience level, and find the job openings that you want.
No surfing required.

VaultMatch Resume Database

Vault takes match-making to the next level: post your resume
and customize your search by area of law, experience and
more. We'll match job listings with your interests and criteria
and e-mail them directly to your inbox.

Alphabetical List of Law Firms

© 2004 Vault Inc.

About the Author

Brook Moshan Gesser

Brook Moshan Gesser is the senior editor at Vault. She holds a JD from the Fordham University School of Law and a BA in English from Vassar College. Before joining Vault, she was a prosecutor for the City of New York.